... AND GOD CREATED SEX

The Salvation Army,
an international movement, is an evangelical part
of the universal Christian church.

Its message is based on the Bible.
Its ministry is motivated by love for God.
Its mission is to preach the gospel of Jesus Christ
and meet human needs in his name
without discrimination.

... *And God Created*
Sex!

CHICK YUILL

Illustrated by
Pascal

THE SALVATION ARMY

MONARCH
Crowborough

British Library Cataloguing Data
A catalogue record for this book is available
from the British Library.

Co-published with The Salvation Army
101 Queen Victoria Street, London EC4P 4EP.

ISBN 1 85424 323 3

Designed and produced by
Bookprint Creative Services
P.O. Box 827, BN21 3YJ, England for
MONARCH PUBLICATIONS
Broadway House, The Broadway,
Crowborough, East Sussex, TN6 1HQ.
Printed in Great Britain

Contents

A Word of Endorsement

This is a 'must read' for every Christian young person. It will make a whole lot of sense to kids who are not Christians, as well. Sex is God's idea – and the God who created it is not a celestial kill-joy wanting to make life miserable for us. But since he made sex, he knows how best to maximise its delights and minimise its dangers.

We seem to have made a pretty miserable mess of sex these days. Most kids who plunge into sexual experience without commitment to a life-long loving relationship find it doesn't live up to its billing. More often than not, it turns out to be more permanent and painful – even dangerous and deadly in its effect – than they bargained for. Maybe it's time we paid attention to the Manufacturer's operating instructions.

Major Chick Yuill walks his readers through the maze of misinformation on sex bombarding young people through music and media, to a satisfying, sane and sensible understanding of human sexuality that is thoroughly Christian and solidly based on God's Word. I want my children and grandchildren to read this one!

General Paul A Radar
International Headquarters
July 1995

1 Sex is a great idea!

IS A GREAT IDEA

A LITTLE BIT OF ARGY-BARGY

'*T*he trouble with you, Dad,' yelled Jenni, 'is that you're old and you don't understand these things!' And with that, the magazine she had been holding – one of those publications aimed at teenagers and devoting a fair amount of space to the subject of sex – suddenly flew across the room and landed at my feet.

That was the cause of the trouble between us. I had just read the article in the latest issue and I was not a happy man. It seemed to be all about how to get hold of the boy of your dreams, how to get him into bed as quickly as possible, and how to avoid getting pregnant in the process. But there was nothing about the things I felt *really* mattered

– the purpose of sex, the quality of relationships, the importance of marriage and family life. And, as dads will, I had made my feelings clear.

A LITTLE BIT OF FAMILY HISTORY

I could see that Jenni and I were about to get into one of those arguments which happen in every family and which usually end up with everybody storming out of the room and nobody being any the wiser, so I decided to remind her that, although I *am* a bit older than she is, I *was* young once and she would not be standing in front of me were it not for an encounter between two very normal and healthy young people.

It was a warm, sunny Sunday morning in the seaside town of Bournemouth in July 1962, the kind of morning when any normal fifteen year old would want to be on the beach. I was normal, fifteen and on holiday, but not, to my annoyance, on the beach. Instead, I was sitting with my folks and my pal Alex in the morning service at the local Salvation Army citadel, enduring rather than enjoying the worship. And then it happened! As the Junior Choir stood to sing, I glanced across the hall and saw her. I guessed that she was probably about the same age as me, and I was convinced that she was the most attractive creature I had ever seen!

I can't remember anything about the rest of the service – nothing about the songs we sang, nothing about the sermon that was preached, nothing except that I tried to keep looking at her without looking as if I was looking! When the service finally ended, two amazing things happened. The first was that, while the rest of the congregation walked out of the building, I floated towards the door, and the second was that when I actually reached the door she was there with her friend waiting to talk to me!

For the two weeks of holiday that followed that Sunday I was on a roller coaster of emotional highs and lows – going out together for the first time, holding hands for the first time, and – bliss beyond words – kissing her for the first time! (I also discovered how fickle girls can be when she came round to the place where we were staying to tell me she didn't want to see me again, only to follow that a couple of days later with a note to say she'd changed her mind.) Then there was the heart-ache of parting when the time came for my family to go back home to Scotland, and all this within the space of fourteen days!

But that was a long time ago, and you are probably wondering what it has to do with you today. Why should you have to join Jenni in listening to a love-story from the dawn of time? Which brings us to the subject of this book. Hundreds of love-letters, scores of arguments, dozens of crises, countless adventures of one kind or another, twenty-five years of marriage, four miscarriages and two healthy daughters later, Margaret and I are still together, still feeling young, still crazy about each other, still enjoying a wonderful physical relationship and still convinced that the life-long commitment of one man to one woman is the perfect pattern for a happy and fulfilling life.

In fact we are so convinced about this and so worried about what we see happening around us that we have long wanted to do something to share what we have learned over the years with younger people. So when the chance of writing this book on one of our favourite subjects came up Margaret said, 'Go for it, Chick!'

A LITTLE BIT OF EMBARRASSING BIOLOGY

Of course, there are some folk who would tell you that what occurred on that Sunday morning in Bournemouth and what has taken place since has no great significance and that I've really gone over the top in describing it as I have done. We're just a higher species of animal with a natural and irresistible urge to reproduce and continue the human race, they will argue. What was really

happening to me was nothing more or less than a surge of my adolescent male hormones. I had reached the stage in my physical development where my body was telling me it was time to mate. It just so happened that the 'chemistry' between Margaret and myself was right.

They will add that all this talk about wedded bliss is ignoring the fact that marriage is just one option among many. Provided you try not to hurt anyone else too much, it's OK to satisfy your sexual urge as and when you want, just as you satisfy your hunger for food. I happened to marry Margaret and stay with her, but I could have had Margaret, Mary and Mandy. Or, since we ought to be free to exercise our sexuality in the way that turns us on, it might even have been Malcolm or Martin!

There are other folk – though not nearly so many these days – who will object to this book for quite different reasons. Sex may be a necessary and unavoidable part of life, they agree. It may even be extremely pleasurable, but somehow it isn't the sort of thing that Christians should be talking about. As one lady who attended one seminar I led put it, 'That's bedroom talk and we don't want to listen to it here!'

To be honest, I grew up with that kind of thinking, and though I wasn't persuaded by it myself, I was quite convinced that it was what Christians ought to believe. Sex was something we all had to do, but it couldn't easily be squared with the things we were supposed to believe and the things we heard preached on a Sunday. Presumably if it happened reasonably quietly in the bedroom at night with the light off it wouldn't upset God too much!

A LITTLE BIT OF ENCOURAGING BIBLE-OLOGY

But, just in case you're starting to think that reading this book isn't such a good idea after all, let me tell you that the truth is quite different. The Bible – contrary to what most people imagine – is really incredibly positive about sex. In fact, I think it is full of good sense about sex and how to enjoy it, and contains a whole load of great stuff that  you can't find anywhere else. Take the story of creation in the early chapters of Genesis, for example. The bit that particularly concerns us at the moment says this:

> Then God said, 'And now we will make human beings; they will be like us and resemble us. They will have power over the fish, the birds, and all animals, domestic and wild, large and small.' So God created human beings, making them like himself. He created them male and female, blessed them, and said, 'Have many children, so that your descendants will live all over the earth and bring it under their control' (Gen 1:26-28).

There are several important truths here for anyone who wants to understand and enjoy their sexuality in a way that will bring them happiness. It is worthwhile pointing them out one by one.

The 'pièce de résistance!'

This passage comes at the end of the account of God's creation of the universe. Human beings are the pinnacle of God's work, his *pièce de résistance*! Not only that, we are actually told that in some wonderful ways human beings are like God. They have consciences and know right from wrong, they have the capacity to enjoy fellowship with God, they can share in his creative work because they have minds and imaginations, and they are entrusted with the control of his world.

This surely means that it is quite wrong to say that we are 'just like other animals'. Physically we are related to the rest of the animal kingdom, but in reality we are 'like God'. We are of a very different order from cats and dogs and elephants. So it is only reasonable that when it comes to our sexual conduct we can expect different standards and values to apply.

Male and female

The next thing to be noticed is that God made human beings 'male and female'. Sex is God's idea! It's a vital part of his design for the universe. And, if you give it just a moment's thought, you will realise that since we are 'like God', there is nothing incompatible between the spiritual and the physical sides of our nature.

Indeed, we can say that there is part of our likeness to

God which can only be seen in our sexuality. Of course, we know that God is pure spirit, that he is not limited by a body, but at different times the Bible describes him as being like either a father or mother. So the fact that we are made in the image of God will be seen in the proper use of our sexual instincts and desires.

It gets better!

If you're finding this encouraging so far, there's more good news for you. It's going to get better still! The first thing God does after he has created human beings, male and female, is to bless them and then say, 'Have many children', or, as the older translations of the Bible put it, 'Be fruitful and multiply.' God's first word to Adam and Eve is a command to get on with it! Wow!

This is all very different from the way in which my Dad spoke to me when he first tried to tell me about sex. He coughed, he shuffled his feet, he looked out of the window,

he blushed, he stammered out a few words – and then he changed the subject! But God handled the matter in a different way. He told them to make love! He didn't have to tell them

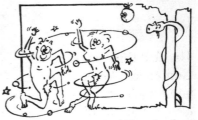

how, of course. When Adam looked at Eve and Eve looked at Adam, their hormones must have been moving even faster than mine did on that Sunday morning in Bournemouth! I guess this was the only commandment that God didn't have to repeat a dozen times to make sure he was obeyed.

I'm not just trying to be funny in all this. There is a very serious point. Have you ever seen one of those cartoons in the newspaper where Adam and Eve are eating the apple from the tree. Usually the snake is crawling off with a wicked look in his eye and Adam and Eve are looking at each other with an expression that leaves you in no doubt that they have just discovered sex.

It would be mildly funny if the message wasn't so dangerous – sex and sin belong together, and if sex doesn't have a little bit of sin in it, then it wouldn't be much fun. But that is a travesty of the truth. When sex and sin get mixed together people get badly hurt. The real truth is that the people who follow God's guidelines are the people who really enjoy sex. God knew and intended that sex would give us pleasure. He also knew that because it is such a powerful force it needs to be kept under control. His guidelines are never negative in intention. They are designed to maximise our happiness and minimise the hurt.

Making love is a serious business!

There is one last point which is so obvious that we might just miss it. Sexual intercourse is the way in which new human beings are created, and there is nothing more serious than bringing a child into the world. That means that personal pleasure must always be balanced with personal responsibility. Making love is the greatest pleasure in the world, but it is also a serious business. It is not wrong to enjoy sex or even to laugh about sex in the right way at the right time. But it is wrong to treat the subject lightly or carelessly. The happiness and safety – indeed the very existence – of other people is at stake here. Be very careful!

AND SO ...

Before we move on, let's just appreciate how generous and loving God is. He could have made sexless human beings, he could have devised a completely boring way of making new people, he could have made sexual intercourse a thoroughly unpleasant experience. But he didn't do any of those things. And we're all glad about that. As a friend of mine once said, 'If God's invented anything better than sex, he's kept it for himself!'

2 One plus one equals one!

Sex, we all agree, is one of God's great ideas. But so are water, and fire, and electricity, and all three have one thing in common with sex. Although they are of tremendous benefit to us, they also have the potential to be extremely dangerous. If they are used in the wrong way, or if they get out of control, they will do inestimable damage. Have you ever seen what happens when a river bursts its banks, or when a fire rages through a building, or when a storm brings down a high-voltage electricity cable? The effect on human life and property can be devastating.

It's like that with sex. It's such a powerful force because the very existence of the human race depends upon our sexual desire, but sex out of control is as dangerous as a raging fire. I can't speak with any authority on how it is for women, but I know from experience that if every man in the world had sexual intercourse on every occasion he felt the urge and with every woman to whom he felt attracted, the complications would be unimaginable. Apart from the damage to people's emotions and the creation of millions of unwanted babies, there wouldn't be time or energy for any other work!

Any reasonable person would expect that a God who came up with the idea of sex would also give his people some guidance on how it should be used. And that is exactly what we find in the Bible. God not only invented sex, he also invented marriage, and marriage is to sex what a well-insulated cable is to a powerful electricity supply. It allows it to be channelled safely for the benefit of everyone.

MARRIAGE AND THE CREATION STORY

Again we need to go right back to the first book of the Bible. There are, in fact, two complementary accounts of the creation of the first man and woman in Genesis. We've already looked at the first one in the previous chapter and discovered how positive God is on the subject of sex. In the second we learn about God's provision of marriage. We pick up the story with the creation of Adam:

> Then the Lord God took some soil from the ground and formed a man out of it; he breathed life-giving breath into his nostrils and the man began to live (Gen 2:7).

So far so good. Everything seems perfect – a beautiful garden, flowing rivers, delicious food in plenty, and Adam is in charge of it all. But there is one problem – he is on his own. So God decides to do something about it:

Then the Lord God said, 'It is not good for the man to live alone. I will make a suitable companion to help him.' So he took some soil from the ground and formed all the animals and all the birds. Then he brought them to the man to see what he would name them; and that is how they all got their names. So the man named all the birds and all the animals; but not one of them was a suitable companion to help him (Gen 2:18-20).

Having provided a perfect world for Adam to live in and an entire zoo for his amusement and supervision, God is still not satisfied. A man needs something more than a dog for company! So the writer of Genesis,  in some of the most beautiful poetry ever written, tells us about God's final and greatest work of creation:

Then the Lord God made the man fall into a deep sleep, and while he was sleeping, he took out one of the man's ribs and closed up the flesh. He formed a woman out of the rib and brought her to him. Then the man said,
   'At last, here is one of my own kind –
Bone taken from my bone, and flesh from my flesh.
"Woman" is her name because she was taken out of man.'
That is why a man leaves his father and mother and is united with his wife, and they become one.
   The man and the woman were both naked, but they were not embarrassed (Gen 2:21-25).

I believe that there are three important truths to be learned from the account of God's provision of Eve as a wife for Adam.

The purpose of marriage

The most obvious thing in the Genesis story is that marriage has been ordained by God for *companionship*. God does not mean us to live solitary lives. There are many good things for us to enjoy in the world, but our greatest need is for human company and the closest human companionship is to be found in marriage.

If you think about it, the story of Eve being made by God out of Adam's rib can only mean one thing: Adam was incomplete as a person until he was given Eve as his wife. When he woke up and found Eve, he was really finding the missing part of himself – and God had turned it into something much more interesting to Adam than a spare rib!

That's how most people feel when they meet their life's partner. It's not for nothing that husbands and wives often speak about their partner as their 'other half'. That's really how it feels. Anyone who knows me knows that without Margaret I'm only half the man I am when she's with me. Later in this book we will have some very positive things to say about people who live a single life, but we can say here, as a general principle, that most of us find a completeness in the deep relationship of marriage that we can find in nothing else and in no other relationship.

If we read a little more closely we will see that the purpose of marriage is particularly focussed in *the act of sexual intercourse*. The man and the woman are to 'become one', or, as the older translations of the Bible render it 'one flesh'. Sexual intercourse between a man and a woman is the deepest expression of love, the closest kind of intimacy, the most serious act of bonding in which two people can take part. It is designed by God to make two separate people into one loving unit. When it comes to sex, God's mathematical formula is: One plus one equals one! Marriage is the place where our powerful sexuality can flow through the channel of committed love. Outside of marriage it is like the river which has burst its banks and the potential for disaster is enormous.

And, of course, though it is not so clearly expressed here as in the passage we looked at in Chapter 1, the companionship and commitment of marriage provide the best human environment for another great purpose – *having and raising children*. Bringing new people into the world is the greatest privilege and the most solemn responsibility that God has entrusted to us. Children thrive best in an atmosphere of loving security and human beings have never discovered anything else which provides that atmosphere like marriage.

The priority of marriage

Because marriage has such an important purpose it has to take *priority* over every other human relationship. As the Bible says, 'a man leaves his father and mother and is united with his wife'. That's a big statement when you think about it. The most important relationship for any young person, even if they don't like to admit it and even if their parents drive them mad at times, is that which they have with their parents. They brought us into the world, they cared for us when we were babies, and we literally owe our life to them. Basic decency demands that we should treat our parents with respect.

But when we get married the relationship with our husband or wife has to replace the relationship with our parents as the number one thing in our lives. As all the mother-in-law jokes remind us, that is sometimes difficult

for parents of newly-weds to understand. The wife who keeps telephoning her mum whenever there is an argument, the husband who tells his wife that she can't cook as well as his mum, the dad who can't let go of his daughter and who continually tells his son-in-law what to do, the mother-in-law who regularly interferes – they're all forgetting that marriage has priority over every other relationship.

Of course, we must still respect our parents. Of course, we should still maintain our links with friends and family, but the forging of a strong relationship between husband and wife and the making of a new family must take first place.

The permanence of marriage

If we were able to read the Old Testament in its original Hebrew language we would discover that when our modern English translations of the Bible speak about a man being 'united' with his wife they are representing a word which describes a bond that is both strong and *permanent*. The Authorised (King James) Version used the good old English word 'cleave' to translate the original.

God's plan for the marriage of a man and woman is that they should form a relationship which can never be broken, that they should 'cleave' to each other, that nothing should ever come between them and cause them to part. Sexual intercourse is so important to God, and so potentially destructive in its power if it is used outside of a loving relationship, that it is his desire that it should only be experienced and enjoyed within the context of a life-long commitment of one man to one woman.

Now, those are pretty strong arguments for marriage and its importance. They should be enough to persuade anyone. But when Jesus came into the world, he brought a whole new dimension to the marriage relationship so that it becomes something more important still. But that's a subject for another chapter.

3 What a picture!

WHAT A PICTURE

One of the remarkable things about Jesus is that he made people see things differently. It wasn't just that he changed how people felt about things that were evil. He also made them look again at good things, things they thought they knew, so that they began to understand them at a deeper level. Certainly that is what happened to Paul after he met Jesus on the road to Damascus. Paul had long been an expert on Jewish life and religion and he never ceased to be either Jewish or religious. But meeting Jesus forced him to reassess his beliefs, to come at them from a different angle and to interpret them in a new way.

Nowhere is that more clearly seen than in what Paul teaches about Christian marriage. As a good Jew, he knew the Old Testament inside out and back to front, and he was more than familiar with all the things we talked about in the previous chapter. But when Jesus became the centre of his life, he realised that marriage was even more important than he had thought. He explains his new picture of marriage in his letter to the Christians at Ephesus. It's two thousand years since he wrote his letter, but his words are still revolutionary enough to change the thinking of everyone who reads and understands them.

A PRINCIPLE FOR ALL RELATIONSHIPS

Paul wants to give these new and inexperienced Christians some guidance on how to handle all relationships, so he makes a general point in his opening sentence before going on to show how it applies to marriage: 'Submit yourselves to one another because of your reverence for Christ' (Eph 5:21).

The first word confronts us with the idea of *submission*. It is, according to Paul, the principle which Christians must follow in all relationships. But don't get the wrong idea and don't imagine that Christians are meant to be

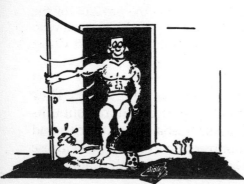

like door-mats, allowing everyone to walk over them! Submission here does not mean 'giving in' to other people, especially if they're in the wrong or if they're behaving like bullies.

Instead, it means simply acting towards the other person with the respect and kindness you would show to Jesus himself if he walked into the room where you are at this very moment. It means that in every relationship and in every encounter you treat other people like you would treat Jesus.

Employers and employees must 'submit' to each other; teachers and pupils must 'submit' to each other; parents and children must 'submit' to each other; friends and colleagues must 'submit' to each other. Why? Because this is the way in which we obey Jesus' command to love one another in the same way that he has loved us (Jn 15:12), and this is the way in which we discover in our everyday experience the truth of his teaching that whenever we act kindly towards even the least important person we are acting kindly towards Jesus himself (Mt 25:40).

If that kind of loving submission – always seeking the best for the other person – is to be displayed in our attitude and actions towards even our most casual acquaintances, then clearly it must be especially important in marriage. And that's what Paul now spells out clearly for us.

A PART FOR WIVES TO PLAY

Wives, submit to your husbands as to the Lord. For a husband has authority over his wife just as Christ has authority over the church; and Christ is himself the Saviour of the church, his body. And so wives must submit completely to their husbands just as the church submits itself to Christ (Eph 5:22-24).

Paul first addresses wives with some startling words. They are to submit to their husbands just as the church submits to Jesus; they are to accept their husbands' authority and they are to give them the honour due to them. Now those are pretty difficult words to swallow. We believe in equality between the sexes and here is Paul talking about women submitting to their husbands. No wonder he often gets a bad press from the feminists!

But that is really a little unfair on Paul, for he, too, believed in equality. In an age that was characterised by barriers of class, race and sex, he went on the record to announce that in the Christian church those barriers had been broken down once and for all. (Look it up for yourself in Galatians 3:26-29.)

So why *does* Paul say what he does? Well, I think there are several reasons. First of all, we have already seen that

'submit' in this context has a very different meaning to the way in which the word is usually understood today. Paul is certainly not suggesting that wives should be tame little creatures who run around at their husband's every whim and attend to his every need! And secondly, the rule is 'submit … to one another', so we can be pretty sure that Paul will be asking husbands to submit to their wives in some way or other.

But, for all that, there is a very clear indication that the husband should be regarded as the head of the family with 'authority over his wife'. That may sound strange to modern 'liberated' men and women, but think about the family situation. Of course, the bringing up of children should be shared by both husband and wife, but because of her biological role in giving birth to the children and in feeding them as babies, the wife will inevitably have a special concern for the 'internal' welfare of the family.

In most families it's Mum who pours oil on troubled waters when there is a disagreement, it's Mum who dries the tears when someone is feeling down in the dumps, it's Mum who knows most clearly when something is not quite right. Dads usually stand back just a little and take a slightly more dispassionate view. They are usually the ones who administer the discipline. They have authority because mums are so busy and so good at being mums.

In addition, in any group of people which has to function as a unit and in which decisions have to be made, *someone* has to have the ultimate authority. Of course, in a good marriage there will be lots of discussion and there will not often be disagreements as to how various matters should be handled.

But inevitably there will be some times when even a husband and wife disagree and that's when someone has to make a decision. According to Ephesians 5:22-24 it should be the husband. Why not the wife? Why should she not have the final say and overrule her husband? Well, most of us – women as well as men, in my experience – seem naturally to dislike that. Why else all those jokes about 'hen-pecked' husbands? We seem to have an inbuilt desire for the husband to exercise the right kind of authority in a marriage.

I don't mean to suggest, of course, that the husband always needs to have the last word or that the wife should not make decisions in matters where she is more competent. In our family, for example, Margaret has always been the one to handle the finances. Since she has a more methodical and mathematical mind than I have, it makes sense for her to do so. Whenever there is a major financial decision to be made, she consults me and I exercise my male authority by saying 'yes' to whatever

she suggests! Seriously, this is an area where the biblical principle needs to be applied with some common sense and with respect for the fact that only a fool insists on having the final say in matters where his wife knows far more than he does.

But there is a more important reason than any of these as to why the husband should have authority and as to where his authority really lies. And that brings us to Paul's words to husbands.

A PART FOR HUSBANDS TO PLAY

Husbands, love your wives just as Christ loved the church and gave his life for it. He did this to dedicate the church to God by his word, after making it clean by washing it in water, in order to present the church to himself in all its beauty – pure and faultless, without spot or wrinkle or any other imperfection. Men ought to love their wives just as they love their own bodies. A man who loves his wife loves himself. (No one ever hates his own body. Instead, he feeds it and takes care of it, just as Christ does the church; for we are members of his body) (Eph 5: 25-30).

If any man reading this passage thinks to himself, 'This is great, I can be in charge while my wife looks after me', then he is in for quite a shock. If wives have to 'submit to their husbands as to the Lord', then husbands have to 'love their wives as Christ loved the church'. In other words, the one to whom the wife must submit is the one who loves her with a love which is so strong that he would literally give his life for her if that was necessary. That is the kind of love Jesus has for us – his church, his body on earth – and that is the kind of love husbands must have for their wives.

Now can you see the kind of authority the husband has to exercise? It is certainly not the authority of the domineering male who regards all females as lesser beings and, therefore, as subservient. Instead, it is the authority of self-giving love, the authority of the one who, by his utter devotion and care, makes his wife into someone even more beautiful than when he first married her.

The perfect example of this kind of transforming love is seen in the life and death of Jesus who changed us from ugly sinners into beautiful saints by his death on the cross. By the same principle, husbands transform their wives not by giving them boxes of cosmetics or by buying them shares in a beauty salon, but by assuring them of their infinite value and worth and by serving them in a spirit of selfless love. The kind of beauty that comes from that kind of love is not just skin deep and it will last even when we are old and grey.

As we suspected, the authority of the husband involves just as much submission as the respect and obedience of the wife. In his case, it is the same as the submission Jesus showed when he allowed himself to be crucified for our sakes. And by now, you can probably see where all this is leading us ....

A PICTURE FOR ALL TO SEE

At the end of the passage from Ephesians which we have been looking at, Paul refers to the teaching about marriage from the creation story which we considered in the previous chapter. And he says something which might seem a little strange to us:

As the scripture says, 'For this reason a man will leave his father and mother and unite with his wife, and the two will become one.' There is a deep secret truth revealed in this scripture, which I understand as applying to Christ and the church. But it also applies to you: every husband must love his wife as himself, and every wife must respect her husband (Eph 5: 31-33).

It seems clear enough to us that the words in Genesis apply to the relationship between a man and a woman in marriage, so why does Paul say that he understands them as applying to the relationship between Christ and the church? If Paul is right, – and we accept his teaching as being inspired by the Holy Spirit – and if these words do apply equally to marriage and to Jesus Christ's relationship with his church, then we must conclude that one of the purposes of marriage, one of the things God wants it to achieve, is to be a living picture of the love between Jesus and his followers. *Good Christian marriages must be one of the most effective means of spreading the gospel.*

To put it as plainly as possible, when people look at our marriage they should be able to see a demonstration of the kind of love God shows to us through Jesus in the way I treat Margaret, and they should see an equal demonstration of our love for Jesus in the way Margaret acts towards me! That's a pretty tall order and we would be the first to admit that we haven't fully achieved that kind of perfection in our marriage. But we are working at it! And if people catch even a glimpse of Jesus in our relationship, we'll be well pleased.

AND SO...

When I think of the companionship and happiness we've enjoyed since we got married, when I think of the pleasure and satisfaction of our physical relationship, and when I think of the privilege and responsibility of making and raising two daughters, I feel really grateful. But when I think that our marriage is meant to be a picture of God's love I feel both humbled and honoured. What a picture! What a privilege!

4 Why wait?

I can almost hear some of you beginning to protest. 'All right,' you say, 'so marriage is wonderful. But I won't be getting married for a while. What do I do now? Everybody else at my school / college / place where I work (delete as appropriate) seems to be having sex every other day. And I'm just as normal as they are. Have I really got to wait until I get married just because I'm a Christian?'

Before I answer your question, let me first of all offer you a bit of wisdom gleaned from years of listening to other people talk about their sexual conquests – *the more a person boasts about what they've done, the less likely it is to be true.* Too many people get pressurised into sexual activity because they want to keep up with the people around them. They think that they must be abnormal because they're not having regular sex and everyone else is. If only

they realised the ...
of lies people tell ...
sex to bolster their ow...
confidence and make them
look good in the eyes of
their friends!

But, having given you
that advice, I'll answer your
question directly with some
bad news. The bad news is – yes, you do need to wait until
you get married. And the good news is – it's worth
waiting for!

We've taken two chapters to talk about marriage so that
you can see how important it is and why sex is best
experienced and enjoyed between two married people.
But you're human, you know what it is to want sex really
badly, and you deserve some convincing reasons as to why
you should wait until marriage. So here goes with some
honest answers to a couple of straightforward questions.
And we'll get the easy one out of the way first.

WHAT ABOUT SEX THAT INVOLVES COERCION?

Sex which involves a degree of coercion – one person
forcing their will on another – is definitely out of order.
When one person forces another to have sex, God's plan is
being turned upside down. Sex is meant to be the supreme
expression of love between two people, but here one
person is using the other person as an object with which to
gratify his or her sexual desire.

That's bad enough in itself, but it's worse still for the
Christian who remembers the words of Jesus when he said
that the way in which we treat others is the way in which
we treat him. The rapist who inflicts pain and degradation
on his victim is also breaking the heart of Jesus.

But before we all get into feeling pious and cosy, let me add that coercive sex doesn't just happen in those terrible cases we read in the newspaper of rape and sexual assault in which physical violence takes place. The young fellow who keeps on at his girlfriend to say 'yes', who tells her that if she loved him she'd sleep with him, and who pressurises her until she gives in, is also guilty of coercion. So is the husband who thinks that his wife is there to provide him with sex on demand with no regard to her feelings. To take away a person's right to say 'no' to sex is one of the cruellest and most evil things one human being can do to another.

WHAT ABOUT CASUAL SEX?

A recent survey by a television programme in the United Kingdom aimed at young people came up with the following statistics regarding casual sex. Of the people they interviewed:

25% of young men and 8% of young women had had 8 or more sexual partners;
42% of young men and 12% of young women had had sex with someone within 24 hours of meeting them;
48% of young men and 28% of young women had been very drunk before having sex.

Even allowing for the fact that we've already noted that people have a tendency to exaggerate when speaking about their sexual encounters, those are worrying figures. Casual sex carries enormous risks. Let me give you some practical reasons why it should be a no-go area.

First, it involves enormous physical risks. There is not only the possibility of an unwanted pregnancy, there is also a real danger of contracting a sexually transmitted disease. In a casual encounter you have no idea of your partner's previous sexual history. As far as the possibility of infection is concerned, you are, in effect, having sex with everyone with whom your partner has ever slept!

And don't believe people who tell you that if you use a condom you're safe. What I'm going to say is so important that I want to get it absolutely right, so I've got one of those little bits of paper in front of me that you find inside a packet of condoms – the bits that give you the instructions and the small print. This is what the largest manufacturers of condoms actually say about their own product:

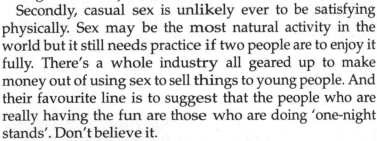

Condoms, used correctly, offer protection against unwanted pregnancy. They can also help provide protection from sexually transmitted diseases, cervical cancer, and HIV/AIDS. However, no method of contraception can provide 100% protection against pregnancy or sexually transmitted diseases.

Safe sex, so called, just isn't safe. It's a big lie. The real truth is that you're dicing with death! On the level of sheer common sense, apart from whether it's right or wrong, casual sex just isn't worth the risk.

Secondly, casual sex is unlikely ever to be satisfying physically. Sex may be the most natural activity in the world but it still needs practice if two people are to enjoy it fully. There's a whole industry all geared up to make money out of using sex to sell things to young people. And their favourite line is to suggest that the people who are really having the fun are those who are doing 'one-night stands'. Don't believe it.

It takes time, practice and an atmosphere of relaxed love

and trust for two people to learn how to satisfy each other sexually. Be on the alert to what is really happening. Young people are being cheated out of what is their right. They're being pressurised to trade a lifelong partnership of increasing sexual satisfaction for a dirty little fumble in an alley or a drunken encounter at a crowded party.

Get wise – don't buy the lie! The people who are having the real fun are not those who have a succession of partners. They are the people who have paid the price of commitment and who are enjoying the returns of their investment in the form of sex that gets better as the years go by.

There's one last practical argument against casual sex and it is this. Sexual intercourse isn't just a physical act. God has so designed us that sexual intercourse involves every area of our personalities, and the hard fact is that if you sleep around you will have to pay a very heavy emotional and physical price. Far from making you feel desirable and glamorous, promiscuous sexual behaviour will actually leave you feeling guilty, shabby and utterly lacking in self-worth. There was one more set of statistics in that survey we quoted earlier and it was this:

> 40% of young men and 49% of young women admitted to having experienced regrets about having sex.

The compilers of the survey were astounded by those figures, but they don't surprise me in the least. In fact, given people's tendency to boast about their sexual prowess and their reluctance to admit when they are wrong, we might well suspect the true figures to be significantly higher. The regret expressed will be greater still for those young people in that survey who move into marriage. One confessed (or claimed!) to have slept with as many as 250 people. What kind of basis can that be for building a relationship in which trust and confidence in each other's integrity is essential?

WHAT DOES THE BIBLE HAVE TO SAY?

It isn't a new problem, of course. The New Testament was written in an age of paganism and promiscuity and in the entire ancient world there was nowhere worse than the

city of Corinth. It was the centre for the worship of Aphrodite, the goddess of love, and at one time 1,000 cult prostitutes served her temple. It was also a seaport where sex-starved sailors would come ashore with one thought on their minds. In fact, the name of the city was synonymous with immorality, and the Greeks – as always – had a word for it: the verb 'to Corinthianise' meant 'to practise sexual immorality'!

No wonder the church at Corinth was beset with problems as its members tried to shake off their old way of life and to come to terms with Christian standards. But when Paul wrote to them he didn't give them a list of 'thou shalt nots'. Instead, he approached the matter positively by showing them how promiscuity was incompatible with a true understanding of what it means to be a Christian. *He gave them a lesson in really safe sex!*

Sexual sin is never right: our bodies were not made for that, but for the Lord, and the Lord wants to fill our bodies with himself. And God is going to raise our bodies from the dead by his power just as he raised up the Lord Jesus Christ.

Don't you realise that your bodies are actually parts and members of Christ? So should I take part of Christ and join him to a prostitute? Never! And don't you know that if a man joins him himself to a prostitute she becomes a part of him and he becomes a part of her? For God tells us in the Scripture that in his sight the two become one person. But if you give yourself to the Lord, you and Christ are joined together as one person.

That is why I say to run from sex sin. No other sin affects the body as this one does. When you sin this sin it is against your own body. Haven't you yet learned that your body is the home of the Holy Spirit God gave you and that he lives within you? Your own body does not belong to you. For God has bought you with a great price. So use every part of your body to give glory back to God, because he owns it (1 Cor 6:13b-20, *The Living Bible*).

Let's compress Paul's teaching into a few sentences that can be easily remembered and used as our slogans in the campaign for *really* safe sex.

Remember who you belong to!

We belong to Jesus Christ and our chief purpose is to serve him. When we became Christians we were spiritually joined to him so that we are his body on earth, doing his work in the world. We've already seen that sexual intercourse involves bonding which is so close that it can only be described as 'one flesh'. That is why Paul poses the startling question, 'Should I take  part of Christ and join him to a prostitute?' If you remember the one to whom you belong, you'll steer well clear of casual sex.

Remember where you're heading!

The pagan religions to which the Corinthians had belonged before they became Christians taught that the physical body was evil and beyond redemption. The way to God was to be found in a kind of mysticism which escaped from the physical to the spiritual realm.

Two conclusions were drawn from that kind of thinking. The first was that what you did with your body didn't matter, and the second was that when you died your soul at last escaped from the body and survived death. To put it bluntly, pagan religion didn't have too high an opinion of the human body.

The Christian gospel is completely different in its teaching on these matters. It insists that God created our bodies in order that we should use them for his glory. In fact, he cares about our bodies so much that when we die he has planned something far greater than the survival of our souls. He will actually remake our bodies in a wonderful way that we cannot fully understand at this moment. We know this is true, because he has promised that he will raise us from death as he raised Jesus.

If your body is as important as all that to God, then you need to be careful how you use it here and now. God is not just interested in spiritual things. He really cares about how you use your sexuality. And casual sex is not part of his will for you! The truth is that you're heading for heaven, not just your soul, but your whole personality – your body as well as your soul.

Remember what you're doing!

Sexual sin isn't the only kind of sin. Nor is it necessarily worse than other sins. I know people who would never dream of getting involved in casual sex, but they wouldn't think twice about hurting others by gossip or destructive criticism. That's at least as bad as sleeping around. And all that we

know about the life and ministry of Jesus in the Gospels assures us that he had a special place in his heart for those who found it difficult to resist sexual temptation.

The real problem with sexual sin, however, as Paul points out, is that 'no other sin affects the body as this one does. When you sin this sin it is against your own body.' What makes sexual sin so terrible is that it involves us in damaging one of God's supreme gifts to us – our physical body – without which we wouldn't have life itself and by which we share in the creation of the lives of others.

Of course, there are other sins – drug abuse for example – which inflict needless and often terrible physical damage on those who commit them. But Paul's point is that sexual sin, involving as it does the most intimate physical and emotional aspects of the human personality, represents a self-inflicted attack on our humanity.

Imagine giving someone you love an expensive gift – let's say a watch – as a token of your deep affection. How would you feel if, immediately on unwrapping the watch, your friend took a hammer, smashed the watch and laughed in your face? I think you'd be feeling just a little bit like God feels when he sees us sinning against our own bodies in some act of sexual promiscuity. If you remember what you're really doing, you'll avoid casual sex like the plague.

Remember why you're special!

Paul is not yet finished as he gives us one good reason after another as to why we should be careful with our bodies. 'Your body,' he now says, 'is the home of the Holy Spirit who lives in you and was given to you by God.' Sexual sin is not just sin against yourself, it is sin against the Holy Spirit who lives in you.

The sense of awe that you feel when you stand in a great cathedral is nothing compared to what you should feel about your own body. You wouldn't dream of vandalising a building that was both a magnificent piece of architecture and a place of worship in which people experienced the presence of God in a special way. So don't even contemplate abusing your own body. Not only is it the wonderful and intricate creation of the Master craftsman, it is the place where the Holy Spirit has resided since the moment you became a Christian.

Remember what you're worth!

Any behavioural psychologist who has studied the matter will tell you that people who get involved in a string of sexual relationships usually have one thing in common – very low sense of self-worth. The very fact that they go from one partner to another is in itself a sure sign that they

are looking for affirmation and affection.

Paul may not have studied modern psychology, but he knew human nature as well as anyone, and he has saved the strongest argument of all to last. 'Your own body does not belong to you. For God has bought you with a great price.'

In other words, remember what you're worth. You don't need to seek personal status in sexual encounters. You are of such enormous value in God's estimation that he was willing to pay the life of his own Son to redeem you from your sin and to bring you back to himself. You are loved and valued, you are a person of eternal significance. Remember that, and don't trade your true value for a second-rate and ultimately unsatisfying sexual encounter.

AND SO ...

Don't be conned by the publicity all around you. A condom is no guarantee of safe sex. It may reduce some of the physical risks but it still leaves you playing a very dangerous game. Take it from me – and from Paul – the only really safe sex is sex that saves itself for someone and something special.

5 But we're in love!

If I was right in my guess that some of you were protesting at the beginning of the previous chapter, then I think that there are probably even louder screams at the beginning of this one. 'Look here,' you're probably saying, 'we accept that it's wrong to force another person to have sex, and we agree with your objections to casual sex. But it's different for us two. We're in love! And we want it really badly. So why shouldn't we go the whole way? It's OK for you, you're married, but you don't understand what it's like for us.'

Before we get down to some hard talking on this one, let

me say that, ancient and married though I am, I *do* still understand. I can remember when we were in love (we still are, but you know what I mean!) and I can remember the times when we wanted to make love every bit as much as you do. I'm really glad now that we didn't, though I have to confess that we had one or two close scrapes. But then we didn't have the benefit of the advice I'm going to give you now! Seriously, I wish that someone had talked to us in a down-to-earth way about how to handle courtship. But nice people and even fiery preachers didn't do that in those days, back in the sixties.

However, fortunately for you, times have changed and I'm going to tell it like it really is. I accept that you're in love. I know there are times when you think you might explode if you don't go the whole way. But it's still better to wait. There's too much at stake to mess this up. So, first I'm going to tell you *why* and then I'm going to tell you *how*.

WE'RE IN LOVE — SO WHY SHOULD WE WAIT?

It's worth waiting because feelings are fickle

If you're really head-over-heels in love, that probably sounds like the most insulting thing anyone has ever said to you. You *know* your feelings are never going to change, you're absolutely sure that you're meant for each other, and you're certain beyond any doubt that you'll never want anyone else. So why wait?

This may not be easy to take, but hear me out. If I had a photograph in this book of every couple who'd said those things to me about their feelings for each other and then changed their minds, you'd be holding the world's biggest photograph album at this moment! People's feelings *do* change – sometimes gradually and sometimes quite suddenly. Maybe they just don't feel like they did about each other any more, or maybe someone else has come along.

Being in love is one of the most wonderful feelings in the world, but by itself it is a notoriously unreliable foundation on which to build a lifelong relationship. Before you're ready to get married – or ready to have sexual intercourse for that matter – you need to have moved on through 'being in love' to commitment, friendship, responsibility and a general sense of realism that allows you to see each other's faults.

Now, don't get me wrong on this one. I still get those feelings for Margaret that I had the first time I saw her, but I don't depend on them and I don't see them as the most important thing. (There's more to be said on the wonder and the danger of being in love, but I'll save it for the chapter called *Fixing the fences*.)

It's worth waiting because discipline pays dividends

Discipline is not the world's most popular subject today. Technology has given us everything from instant coffee to instant information. That's OK and it makes life easier in many ways. But inevitably, people tend to want the same principle of instant results to apply in the area of personal relationships. 'I want it and I want it now' is the motto of the age we live in. Discipline is hard work, especially when it comes to sex. Instant sexual gratification may well be the message beamed at us non-stop by the media, but it's a philosophy which does great damage in the long term. Let me tell you of two ways in which discipline pays dividends.

Discipline pays dividends because it *puts your love to the test*. It's the easiest thing in the world to say, 'I love you, so let's go to bed.' It's far more difficult to say, 'I love you and I'll prove it by my respect and the fact that I'm willing to wait.' An attitude like that will soon begin to indicate whether what you have between you is just a passing attraction or whether it is something that will develop into the basis of a lasting relationship. I promise you this, if you're really meant for each other, your love will grow far richer by waiting than by leaping into bed together.

But not only does discipline act as a test of your love here and now, it also *builds up trust* for the future. I can best explain what I mean by telling you something very personal. I know that I can trust Margaret anywhere, at any time and with any man – however attractive she might find him. Why? Because I know how much she wanted to make love with me before we got married and I know how much discipline she developed by not doing it. If she wouldn't do it for me outside marriage, I am 100% sure she won't ever do it with anyone else. And she trusts me for exactly the same reason. Enough said!

It's worth waiting because sex alone isn't sufficient

Several hundred years ago, when he was still young, Cliff Richard made a movie for World Wide Films. I can't recall the title but I do remember one scene in which Cliff was trying to persuade his girlfriend to have sex with him. She refused, so Cliff got mad at her and said, 'What's wrong with you? You love me, don't you? Surely it's not much to ask!' And she replied, 'That's the problem, you're not asking enough. I want to give you everything and you want to settle for a dirty fumble in the grass.'

I don't know who wrote the screenplay for that movie, but they got it absolutely right. The problem is that sex

before marriage gives you far less than it promises. Sex works best as part of a total package – loving each other, making a commitment to each other, building a home together, planning a family, getting to know each other intimately, working through good times and bad – and when you try to have it by itself it's a surprisingly unsatisfying experience.

The best analogy I can think of at this moment is that it's a bit like the time when I was a kid and I found one of my Christmas presents. It was more than a week before 25th December, but I knew how wonderful it was to open presents. I knew I really shouldn't, but I gave in to temptation. The present was a superb one, but somehow it wasn't the same. I'd opened it outside of the proper context of Christmas Day with all its atmosphere and magic and I had a kind of empty, unsatisfied feeling inside. I never did it again. There's a wonderful magic to sex within marriage. Don't spoil it by opening the present too soon.

WE'RE IN LOVE – SO HOW CAN WE WAIT?

That's all very well, but you're now asking, 'How do we manage it? How can two healthy people who really love

each other conduct a normal relationship without having sex?' Well oddly enough, it's the same answer you'd get to the question, 'How do porcupines make love?' – with great difficulty! It's not easy but it can be done and it's well worth the effort. And I want to give you the kind of honest help that we didn't have when we were dating. So, here are five rules to take at least some of the wanting out of waiting.

Keep away from the edge!

Let me explain what I mean by that. The question all young people want to ask when you encourage them to wait is this: 'How far can we go?' But that's the wrong question and I'll tell you why. Every year, around the coast of the United Kingdom there are tragedies that could be avoided. People fall from cliff edges just because they go too close to the edge. So when the authorities put up a fence to protect us from our own curiosity and stupidity they don't ask, 'How close can we put the fence to the edge of the cliff?' They ask, 'How far away from the edge can we put this fence without spoiling the view and without unduly restricting public access?'

I'm sure you can see the point I'm making. If you keep going as close to the edge as you possibly can, one day you're likely to slip and fall over. And if you keep going as far as you can with your partner, doing everything you can think of except actually having intercourse, one day you're bound to slip and go all the way.

It's far better to have a few good rules – clearly understood by both yourself and your partner – that keep you well away from the edge. Then, when you get carried away a little and go a bit further than you meant to – as we're all liable to do – you'll still be well short of full sexual intercourse. So, here's how to keep your fence in good repair....

Keep your friends around!

All couples need to spend time alone with each other. If you don't, there's something wrong with your relationship and you'll never really get to know each other. But, having said that, it's also true that too many

couples spend far too much time on their own. If you do that, two things happen: firstly, however much you're in love, you get bored and run out of things to say and do; and secondly, you get to thinking about just one thing – and you've already guessed what that is! If you've got nothing to occupy your brain, it won't be long until your body takes over.

So keep your friends around. Enjoy going out in a group. Apart from the fact that it will keep your relationship from becoming too physically intense, you'll find that you argue a lot less and that you appreciate the times you do spend just with each other all the more.

Keep your feet on the floor!

It is one of the most firmly attested scientific facts in the entire universe that when two people of the opposite sex lie down on a bed together their brains immediately send a message to their bodies saying, 'Over to you, now!' and then switch off completely. It is equally well attested that their bodies act on this instruction without any delay and begin marshalling millions of hormones, every one of which has the word SEX stamped across it in large luminous letters!

There is no way you are going to manage to wait until marriage if you regularly lie down on a bed together. I don't care if you are just listening to music or reading a book, and I don't care if you just lie on top of the bed and don't get under the covers. A bedroom is a red-alert area and a bed is a ticking sexual timebomb. Be sensible – keep your feet on the floor and your brains upright and intact. It will save you from all sorts of problems.

Keep your clothes on!

This one's so obvious that you'd think it doesn't need saying. But you'd be amazed – on second thoughts, you probably wouldn't – at how many Christian courting couples want to go as far as undressing each other. The

effects of this activity on any normal young and healthy person are so obvious that I'm not going to spell them out for you. If you can't think what they are, you're wasting your time reading this book and I suggest that you get hold of *Train-spotting for Teenagers* or *Crochet for Beginners*. They'll be much more on your wavelength than a book like this!

Keep your hands off!

I've no idea why kissing is such an unbelievably pleasant thing to do. When you think about it, it's both very silly and very unhygienic. Of course, when you're kissing, you're not thinking about it, you're just *doing* it! The only problem is that when you're close enough to kiss, your arms and hands tend to get in the way, so either you wrap them round each other or you find things for them to do – and that's where the trouble usually starts!

You need a rule for your hands if you're going to survive until marriage and the best one I know is the one that Steve Chalke teaches. (In case you don't know who Steve is, he's a Baptist pastor in England, and an expert communicator with young people, and he's much too handsome for his own good. Something should be done about people like that! He's also produced an excellent video called *Lessons in Love* which is well worth seeing.)

Anyway, Steve's rule here is, *Whatever parts of the body your partner has that you don't have – keep your hands off them!* That may be blunt and to the point but it's excellent advice.

I could expand on it by telling you all about erogenous zones and tactile stimulation and all that kind of stuff. But I won't bother, because I'd just be giving fancy names to things you know as well as I do. It's sufficient to say, that your body is 'wired up' in such a way that some parts get you going as soon as they're touched in a loving kind of way. I'm sure your imagination is already running riot, so we'll leave the subject quickly ...

AND SO ...

Those are my five basic rules for anyone who wants to know how to save the best for marriage. Like I say, it isn't easy, especially when you really love someone. But it is worthwhile. And I give you my promise that, ten or twenty years down the road, you'll be glad you waited. But I'm beginning to sound old and sensible, and if I'm not careful you won't read any further. Come to think of it, though, I'd rather be old and sensible than old and sorry ....

6 Who needs a piece of paper?

A CHANGE IN ATTITUDE

So far we've said a great deal about how important marriage is. We have to accept, however, that not everyone would agree with us. In fact, there is an increasing number of young people who are 'voting with their feet' on this issue. Cohabitation – living together without getting married – is the order of the day for many in our society. 'Who needs a piece of paper?' they ask. 'It's the quality of the relationship that really matters, not whether you've gone through a ceremony or not.'

All too often, Christian leaders have just raised their

hands in horror at such words. But that will not do. We need to understand why so many young people feel as they do, in order that we can explain why cohabitation is an unsatisfactory alternative to marriage. I want to suggest that there are three main reasons for the change in attitude.

A loathing of hypocrisy

First, young people have a healthy loathing of hypocrisy. I have to admit that I can understand their impatience with much of what they see around them. There are too many marriages that are empty of love, there are too many  marriages that end in the divorce court, and young people particularly are totally fed up with hypocrisy like that.

What's more, they're absolutely right that no ceremony by itself makes a good relationship. You can spend a small fortune on a wedding with all the trimmings and still end up with all the pain of separation if you're not prepared to give marriage the hard work it needs and deserves.

A loss of faith

Secondly, there is a general loss of faith in society at large. Surveys show that, whilst the majority of people may have a vague belief in God, it does not affect the way they live. They certainly don't look to the Bible for guidance as to right and wrong. The retreat from marriage is one symptom of a larger problem. The majority of people have no firm beliefs and, consequently, they have no rules for how they should behave.

A lack of commitment

Thirdly, there is a lack of commitment in our society which is linked to the loss of faith, but which also owes much to an overall uncertainty about life in general. For half a century we have lived with the constant threat of the annihilation of the human race by nuclear weapons; the present generation lives under the shadow of the AIDS epidemic; and the harsh reality of years of unemployment stares many young people in the face. No wonder that so many people view every aspect of life only in the short term. What is the point in long-term commitments when life is a game of chance played out in a world that could be blasted into smithereens at any moment?

In the present climate of moral confusion and deep-seated pessimism, the trend towards cohabitation is understandable. But for all that, marriage is still the best way, it is still God's way, and it is no exaggeration to say that in an uncertain world it is the only sure way if we want to find lasting happiness for ourselves, security for our children, and stability for society at large. But it is no use simply preaching that cohabitation is wrong. It is time to go on the attack and to present the case for marriage. Let's ask two basic questions that will help us to do just that.

What makes a good relationship?

What's so important about a wedding ceremony?

WHAT MAKES A GOOD RELATIONSHIP?

Consent

The most obvious thing about a healthy relationship is that there must be consent. Both parties need to be agreed that they want

to spend their lives together. That applies even in societies and cultures where parents choose a husband or wife for their daughter or son. Although the young people don't make the choice themselves, they do consent to abide by the choice that has been made and to work at their marriage.

To us in the West, that may well seem a strange way of doing things, but it has to be said that, for all our supposed freedom, it's too easy to be pushed into a marriage by peer pressure ('everyone's married by the time they're your age') or to be carried along by romantic notions without having given the matter serious consideration. Real consent means that you've thought the relationship through, you've faced up to the things you don't like in your partner, and you've recognised that marriage is going to mean a lifetime of hard work.

Commitment

That leads us on to commitment. Any sensible person can see just how important that is. A society in which people move easily and rapidly from one sexual partner to another is a society which will soon be in chaos. The damaging effects of such short-term relationships on children is being documented increasingly by observers of contemporary life.

People who move thoughtlessly from one relationship to another are usually low on maturity and high on selfishness. A good relationship depends on two people who enter it with the serious intent of making it work, and who sustain it with a determination to stick by each other through thick and thin.

Contract

Then, there has to be some form of contract, either formal or informal. If two people are to live and work together for any length of time, each needs to know what the other expects and  each needs some kind of protection from being exploited by the other. Even if they choose just to live together with no formal marriage contract, there has to be some kind of verbal agreement about various practical aspects of the relationship – who pays the bills, who owns their home or is responsible for the rent, who makes decisions about having children and how those children should be brought up, what is to happen to property in the event of a break-up in the relationship. There has to be some kind of contract in any relationship which has a degree of permanence.

Consummation

Finally, a good relationship between a couple must be consummated in the act of sexual intercourse. Of course, it is *possible* for two people of the opposite sex to live together in a purely platonic

relationship, but that would be very unusual and very different from the kind of relationship we are talking about. A healthy and satisfying sex life is crucial to the quality of any lasting and committed relationship between a man and a woman.

WHAT IS SO IMPORTANT ABOUT A WEDDING CEREMONY?

Before we answer this question directly, there are a couple of things we need to make clear. In the first place, when we talk about a wedding ceremony we mean a Christian ceremony. Many people go through a civil marriage service and whilst we would not denigrate that in any way, it is not the same as a Christian marriage ceremony. Inevitably, it focuses on the contract element of the relationship and it does not have the 'high' view of marriage that we have presented in this book.

Years ago, C. S. Lewis, one of the most astute Christian commentators of this century, suggested that there should be two distinct kinds of marriage – one, organised by the civil authorities which would be for all citizens, and the other, presided over by the church which would be for Christians. We have not quite reached that point, but the difference between Christian and 'secular' marriage is very real.

The second thing we need to make clear is that very often the things that *seem* to be most important about weddings are not really important at all. Dinner suits and long white dresses, riding in Rolls–Royce cars, elegant photograph albums, expensive meals in classy hotels – these things are all very well, but they have nothing to do with what really matters. Indeed, a strong case could be made for the fact that they actually get in the way and obscure the things that are important.

Of course, every couple wants their wedding day to be special and that is only right. But perhaps we need to be asking questions about the expense and even extravagance of some wedding receptions. It's even become one of the arguments people now use for cohabitation – 'We would get married, but we can't afford to do it properly'! A wedding can and should be both a dignified and a significant occasion without costing the earth. Apart from anything else, in a world where millions are starving, Christians should be asking serious questions about unnecessary extravagance.

Now we are in a position to answer our question, 'What is really important in a Christian wedding ceremony?' I have thought long and hard about this and I've come up with the following answer:

A Christian wedding ceremony is important because on a particular day the couple make their solemn promises to each other in the presence of God, in an atmosphere of prayer, and in a public act of commitment.

Let's break that sentence down bit-by-bit in order to grasp its full meaning.

... On a particular day ...

It seems that in every society people have a need to mark significant changes in life with ceremonies or events which both highlight the importance and help to explain the meaning of those changes. That is certainly true for Christians. The arrival of a baby is marked by a christening or dedication. The fact that a young person has reached a level of maturity which allows them to accept the Christian faith for themselves is marked by confirmation in some church traditions, by adult believers' baptism in others, and, of course, by a swearing-in as a senior soldier in The Salvation Army.

When someone dies we don't just dispose of the body – we have a funeral service in order that the family and friends of the deceased can express their sadness, show proper respect to the one they have lost, and begin to come to terms with their grief. Such 'rites of passage', as they are sometimes called, are far more than just old rituals. They act as signposts on the journey of life, marking out the important events on our journey from the cradle to the grave.

It seems odd, then, that many people move into the most important relationship in life without any proper ceremony to mark the event. From where I sit typing these words I can see our wedding photograph which hangs on the wall as a reminder of Saturday 28th September 1968. That date and the events of that 'particular day' are etched on my memory. It is a key point in our lives and in the story of our family. Everything that happened served to emphasise the fact that we were embarking on a relationship that was sacred and special and 'for keeps'.

I'm pretty sure that if we had just 'drifted into' living together, it would have been relatively easy just to have 'drifted out' again! But the fact that our marriage had a definite beginning in which its meaning and purpose were so clearly declared has served to strengthen our resolve to make it work in good times and in bad. I am grateful beyond words for that 'particular day'.

... the couple make their solemn promises to each other ...

The main reason for that day was, of course, that we should have an opportunity to promise each other to be faithful as long as we lived. The full wording of the marriage ceremony used in The Salvation Army is printed in an appendix at the end of this book. (I've used this particular version of the marriage ceremony because I am a Salvation Army officer, because that is the version with which I am most familiar,

and because many readers of this book will belong to that part of the Christian church. But I am sure that everyone else will find it relevant and not too dissimilar to what is used in other churches.)

If you read the wording through carefully you will see that three of those things we identified as being vital to a good relationship come together in these promises. There is clear *consent* as both partners openly declare that they wish to be married and that there are no reasons to prevent that happening. Since they will have attended marriage preparation classes leading up to the wedding, they will have thought very carefully about every aspect of marriage. Their consent will not just be the product of a strong attraction to each other; it will have been tested in informed discussion.

There is also an unequivocal *commitment* to each other as they promise:

> to have and to hold
> from this day forward,
> for better for worse,
> for richer for poorer,
> in sickness and in health,
> to love and to cherish,
> till death us do part …

There is nothing vague about those words. No intelligent person can hear them without being aware that Christian marriage requires a life-long commitment of each partner to the other.

And there is a *contract* which is freely entered into. In a Christian marriage ceremony the couple enter into a new relationship not only in the eyes of God and of the church, but also in the eyes of the law. Each promises to take the other as 'my lawful wedded' husband or wife, and the contract is sealed by the exchange of rings, accompanied by the words:

> I put this ring upon your finger
> as a continual sign that we are married
> under the solemn promises
> we have made this day …

It is those promises of commitment for life, freely made and issued in the contract of marriage, that provide the secure environment within which the relationship can be *consummated* in the act of sexual intercourse. When two people have sincerely made such vows to each other, then sex can take place in an atmosphere which is free from guilt or anxiety, the kind of atmosphere of love and trust in which it works best.

*... in the presence of God
...*

A Christian marriage
ceremony is first and
foremost an act of worship
– it takes place in
the presence of God.
Cohabitation involves two
partners living together,
but Christian marriage
involves three parties – a
man, a woman, and God.
That makes all the
difference. If two people

live only for each other, then that relationship, however
loving, can become selfish. But when marriage takes place
in the presence of God, when he is given first place, the
danger of selfishness is overcome by a spirit of service. As
The Salvation Army Articles of Marriage put it:

> We do solemnly declare that, although we enter into this
> marriage for reasons of personal happiness and fulfilment, we
> will do our utmost to ensure that our married status and
> relationship will deepen our commitment to God and
> enhance the effectiveness of our service as soldiers of Jesus
> Christ in The Salvation Army.
>
> We promise to make our home a place where all shall be
> aware of the abiding presence of God, and where those under
> our influence shall be taught the truths of the gospel,
> encouraged to seek Christ as Saviour, and supported in the
> commitment of their lives to the service of God.
>
> We declare our intention to be to each other, by the help of
> God, true Christian examples and, through times of joy,
> difficulty or loss, to encourage each other to 'grow in grace
> and in the knowledge of our Lord and Saviour Jesus Christ'.

You might sum up those words by saying that, when a couple make their promises in the presence of God, they are announcing that their marriage is at least as much about being of service to God and humanity as it is about being in love with each other.

... in an atmosphere of prayer ...

Whenever I conduct a wedding ceremony, the first thing I do immediatley I have pronounced the couple to be man and wife, is to ask them to kneel. I then lay my hands on them both and pray that the Holy Spirit will fill their lives and enrich their relationship with the love of God. I believe that God always answers that prayer and that special blessing is given to each couple on their wedding day.

But in asking them to kneel, I want to do something more than simply pray for them there and then. I am trying to emphasise to the couple themselves and to their family and friends that their entire marriage should be lived out as it has begun – in an atmosphere of prayer. I want them to pray together regularly and to know that all the power and grace of God is available to them in every circumstance of life.

If you begin a thing properly, it is much easier to continue properly. Nutritionists will tell you that people who have a healthy breakfast get a better start to the day than those who don't take the trouble to eat properly. The relationship between a man and a woman is no different. If it starts with prayer it is all the more likely to continue with prayer. If the blessing of God is sought right at the start it is all the more likely to be sought and enjoyed all the way through.

... in a public act of commitment

A marriage ceremony can, of course, take place in private,

but that is not the normal practice, and there are several significant reasons why a wedding is conducted in the presence of family and friends. The most obvious one is that when we make a public statement *it strengthens our resolve*.

Some years ago I was appointed to a corps – that's the name Salvation Army folk give to their local church – where the hall was old and no longer suitable for the kind of ministry we needed to carry out in the area. So after a few weeks I called a meeting and announced to everyone that during our time of leadership in that place we would make sure that a new hall was built. There were times when there seemed to be little progress and when I almost wished I'd kept my big mouth shut! But the fact that I had made a public promise meant that I couldn't give up. The public promises we made at our wedding have strengthened our resolve in just the same way.

Not only is our resolve strengthened by the fact that marriage vows are made publicly, but we also *secure the support of others*. When I promised my congregation that I would do everything in my power to secure a new building, they responded by saying, 'If you're willing to make that promise we'll work and pray with you to make it come true.'

It was the same on our wedding day. People were saying

to us by their presence, 'We will give you all the help we can to make your promises come true.' And many of them have honoured that promise over the years with their prayers, their friendship, their advice, their hospitality, and even, on occasions, with gifts of money. I'm sure that our experience is no different from that of many other couples.

There is one more benefit from the public commitment of the marriage ceremony and that is that our promises *serve to encourage others*. I can illustrate it again from my promise to build a new hall. People who'd become fed up waiting for something to happen regarding the property, suddenly felt encouraged; they made a new commitment to the financial giving and fund-raising which were needed.

A wedding ceremony works like that. There will be married people there who will be reminded of their own wedding day and who will silently renew their vows. There will be young couples present who will realise the importance and significance of marriage for their own future. 'No man is an island' wrote John Donne, and he was right. Everything we do affects other people in some way or another, and few things have a more powerful encouraging effect than a marriage ceremony which is conducted with dignity and in which solemn promises are made joyfully, sincerely and publicly.

THE LAST WORD

Margaret and I have the privilege of ministry in a part of the Christian church which is probably unique in that it was founded not by one man but by a married couple – William and Catherine Booth. Their courtship and marriage make up one of the great love stories of all time. So it is appropriate that the last word should go to Mrs

Catherine Booth. A few days after their engagement on 15th May 1852, Catherine wrote a letter to her fiancé. The language may be a little old-fashioned, but it is not difficult to understand, and it captures perfectly the privilege and purpose of Christian marriage.

> The thought of walking through life perfectly united, together enjoying its sunshine and battling with its storms, by softest sympathy sharing every smile and every tear, and with thorough unanimity performing all its momentous duties, is to me exquisite happiness; the highest earthly bliss I desire. And who can estimate the glory to God and the benefit to man accruing from a life spent in such harmonious effort to do his will? Such unions, alas, are so rare that we seldom see such an exemplification of the divine idea of marriage ...
>
> The more you lead me up to Christ in all things, the more highly shall I esteem you; and if it be possible to love you more than I now do, the more I shall love you.

Those who trade this unique combination of being in love with each other and being of service to God for mere cohabitation are making the worst bargain of their lives.

7 Fixing the fences

We've been insisting that marriage is God's great idea, the setting for a life of happiness and sexual fulfilment. But if you take a look around you, it won't be long before you realise that something is badly wrong. In the affluent Western world somewhere between a third and a half of all marriages end in separation and divorce. And every one of those divorces means real unhappiness for the couple, confusion and hurt for any children involved, and serious problems for society at large.

Christians, of course, are not immune to what is happening around them, and an increasing number of Christian couples are experiencing the heart-break and trauma of divorce. Every marriage is under constant threat today. So, even though many of you reading this book are not yet married, it is never too early to learn. As the man said, 'Forewarned is forearmed!'

Entire books could be – and have been – written on the subject, but here in the space of one short chapter is a set of simple instructions on how to fix the fences so that you can protect your marriage and keep temptation and break-up at bay.

TAKE TIME!

Take time to think

If marriage is meant to last a lifetime, then clearly it is important to take time to get it right! In the first place, you need to take time to think before you get married. Too many marriages go wrong because they should never have happened at all. I said in Chapter 5 that I'd have more to say about the wonder and the danger of 'being in love', and it's time to return to the subject now.

Being in love is not by itself sufficient reason for getting married. The very strength of your emotions can blind you to all kinds of other things that need to be considered. For example, is there something about your partner that worries you or that you really don't like? If there is, you need to stop and think whether marriage is going to be right, however much you feel in love.

And don't fall into the trap of saying, 'Well, yes there is a problem, but I'm sure things will change after we get married.' That never works; people don't change in that way. If your boyfriend or girlfriend has a vicious temper, or a serious problem with alcohol, or continually gets into debt, those things won't disappear magically on your wedding day. If they can't be sorted out before marriage, the chances are slim that they'll resolve themselves afterwards. Apart from serious shortcomings such as those to which we've just referred, you need to ask yourself whether your personalities, your different likes and dislikes, your hopes and expectations are such that you can envisage spending the rest of your life together.

Whenever I am counselling a couple in preparation for marriage, I have one question that I always ask them, even though I know it is almost impossible to answer: 'If you were to find out today that your fiancé had a serious illness which meant that he or she would spend the rest of their life seriously disabled, would you still want to go through with this marriage?'

Only if the answer is 'Yes', only if you have reached that kind of commitment which goes far deeper than feelings, should you get married. So you'd better take time to think!

Take time to talk

It's amazing how quickly two people who began their marriage with feelings of intense love for each other can grow apart. Good communication is vital if a marriage is to last. Couples need to take time to talk – and, even more important, to listen – to each other! They need to talk about what they've been doing each day; they need to talk about any difficulties they are experiencing in their relationship; they need to talk about how they are budgeting their money; they need to talk about how many children they want to have and when they want to have them; they need to talk about their Christian commitment; they need to talk about how they are going to allocate their time between work, family, leisure and Christian service.

It is no exaggeration to say that every problem in a marriage is at root a problem in communication. And it is equally true that there is almost no difficulty which cannot be overcome when two people talk, listen, and seek to reach an amicable and fair compromise.

There are even times when it might well be necessary for both partners to talk to someone else about difficulties in their marriage. I don't mean, of course, the kind of thing that happens when the wife is always running home to mum to complain about her husband or when the husband moans about his wife to his pals. I'm thinking, rather, of the situation where a couple will talk together to a good friend they can trust, or to a skilled, professional counsellor who knows how to listen with care and direct with gentleness.

The interesting thing is that often when a couple talk through their difficulties together in this way they don't need good advice. As they listen and speak common-sense solutions often become apparent. Many a marriage that has ended in disaster could have survived and flourished if both partners had been humble enough and honest enough to seek help and to admit that all was not well.

Take time to pray

I have one great fear about Christian marriages and it is this: I suspect that the majority of Christian couples spend little time – if any – in prayer, either alone or with each other. I might be quite wrong on this one, of course, but all I can tell you is that I've often mentioned it when I've been preaching over the last ten years, and I've always added that if I'm wrong I'd be grateful for someone to come and challenge me at the end of the meeting. To date no one has ever done so – and I've never found folk to be backwards in coming forwards when they think the preacher has got something wrong!

If marriage is to work as God intends, then you need to take time to pray. We don't have space in a book like this to give detailed guidance on prayer – there are many other excellent books which will help you in that vital subject. It is enough for us to note here that prayer does two great things for a couple.

First, it involves God in the marriage. Far from struggling through on their own, the couple who pray with each other and for each other have all the love and power of God at their disposal. Two people and God represent a mighty force!

Secondly, it makes it very difficult to sustain a quarrel. There is something about praying together that makes you want to say, 'I'm sorry, let's put this right now.' It's an experience that's related to what Jesus taught in his prayer: 'Forgive us our trespasses as we forgive those that trespass against us.'

You can't come into the presence of God if you're feeling bitterness against another person, especially someone as close to you as your husband or wife. Talk to God together, and you'll soon be talking to each other, however big a quarrel you've had!

Just one last word on this subject before we move on: if you're engaged, or even if you're just courting and you think your relationship might develop into something lasting, it's never too early to start to pray together. Most people actually find it a bit embarrassing the first time they try it, so let me offer you some assorted bits of advice on this one:

> Don't get all religious and 'close your eyes and bow your heads'. (To tell you the truth, I've no idea why we make such a big deal about closing our eyes when we pray. I usually fall asleep when I do that!) It's actually much easier if you just imagine God is sitting next to you – which, in a sense, is true – and talk to him as naturally as you would to each other.
>
> Remember, just talking things through in the presence of God is a kind of prayer.
>
> Try reading a short passage from the Bible together and then discussing what it means for you both.
>
> And finally … it doesn't matter if you get a fit of the giggles in the middle of a time of prayer together. In fact, I'm pretty sure that God much prefers that to some of the dreary piety that often passes for prayer.

TAKE CARE

It's time to talk about 'being in love' again! We've already pointed out that being in love is not, by itself, sufficient reason for getting married. Now we need to put something else right. If you think that once you've fallen in love that's it, that you'll never be attracted to anyone else – you're making a BIG mistake!

I read somewhere that a Christian psychologist had pointed out that a normal, healthy adult could fall in love seven or eight times in one lifetime. I don't know a lot about psychology, but I am a normal, healthy adult and I'm sure he's dead right! And there's no point in you threatening to tell Margaret, because she knows and she tells me it's been just the same for her!

Contrary to what you read in romantic novels and see in the movies, falling in love is *not* an irresistible emotion. If I believed that nonsense, I might well be on my fourth or fifth marriage by now. Of course, that's assuming that the person to whom I was attracted felt the same about me! And I never found that out. Why? Because I made sure that they didn't know and that I never allowed those feelings to take over.

I have a relationship with Margaret which is not based on feelings but on an act of commitment on which there can be no going back. And I've learned that some feelings need to be sent on their way while I turn my attention to more healthy matters. In short, I've learned to *take care*. Again, let me boil it down to a couple of simple but indispensable guidelines which I've picked up over the years.

Take care of each other

I have a motto on this matter which people sometimes find amusing, and this is it: 'People who get steak at their own table don't go stealing hamburgers from other people's kitchens.' We'll have more to say on this towards the end of this chapter, but the point is worth making now – the couple who take care of each other, who enjoy their sexual relationship, who take time to express their love will be far less vulnerable to temptation than the couple who neglect each other and who need, therefore, to find affection and reassurance elsewhere.

Take care to keep out of temptation

Years ago the evangelist Billy Graham made a rule for himself; he determined that he would never travel alone in a car with any woman other than his wife. Now some folk think that's going 'over the top', and that there's no need to go to such extremes. But the interesting thing is that, whereas some of his fellow evangelists have fallen into serious sexual sin and have brought a great deal of discredit on the gospel they preach, Billy Graham's ministry has never suffered from even a hint of scandal.

The fact is that Billy Graham is just following the simple maxim: if you take care of how things look, then you take care of how things are. It makes a lot of sense. So, for example, as a Salvation Army officer, I never visit young ladies on my own; I don't get involved in counselling widows or other women whose grief or distress might make both of us vulnerable; and – on a very practical level – when I'm in the office with my assistant, a delightfully attractive young lady, the door is always kept ajar. That means that not only can anyone enter at any time without wondering what we might be up to, but also that I am not putting myself in a situation where I might easily be at risk from temptation.

Do you remember the story of Joseph in the house of Potiphar? (If you don't, check it out in Genesis 39.) Potiphar was a highly placed government official and his wife was the archetypal bored upper-class housewife with too much time on her hands. Not to put too fine a point on it, she wanted to get to know Joseph better – and she was far more interested in his body than his mind!

Joseph tried to reason with her at first, but it was no use – she was determined to make Joseph the first 'toy-boy' in history. So one day, when she made a pass at him and grabbed him by his robe, Joseph decided the time had come to make a sharp exit. Mrs Potiphar kept hold of his robe, but he was out of the door and safely away from the reach of temptation.

Many a tragedy could have been averted and many a marriage could have been saved if men and women had followed the example of Joseph throughout the centuries and kept out of the way of temptation. If I was an alcoholic, I wouldn't take a job in a brewery to prove the power of God to give me victory over temptation! Instead, I'd use the common sense he's given me to keep away from alcohol.

In just the same way, I recognise how vulnerable I am to sexual temptation and I take care of how things look, I take care of how things are, and I don't put myself in temptations where my body might start to take over from my brain.

MAKE LOVE

But let's end this chapter on a positive note. The best way to build the fences around a marriage is to make love all day long – from morning till night! In my imagination I can hear a cheer go up around the world from every reader of this book, but before you get too excited I'd better explain what I mean. When I talk about 'making love' I'm talking about something more than sexual intercourse, though, of course, that's a vital element in love-making. I'm using the phrase in its literal sense – making love, creating an atmosphere of love between two people.

Truth to tell, the reason so many couples have an unsatisfying sex life is that they think love-making suddenly happens when you enter the bedroom. In fact, in a marriage that is really working that's just the climax – no pun intended – of a whole series of caring, loving acts. Making love actually begins the moment you wake up in the morning and depends on all those little loving looks, touches and actions that go to make a good relationship.

Let me give you ten commandments for couples who want to make love from morning till night.

1 Make sure you say 'I love you' to each other every day. I know you can argue, 'But she knows I love her.' That may well be true, but she – or he – needs to hear you say it. And as you speak out the words they reinforce and strengthen your feelings and your commitment.

2 When you're annoyed about something it's far better to say so than to bottle it up inside. No couple wants to be constantly arguing, but a blazing row is far healthier than simmering resentment. However, when you've had an argument like that, always be the first to say 'I'm sorry'. It really is true that it's almost worth having a row just for the sheer pleasure of making up again.

3 Always share the tasks that have to be done at home. Nobody ever feels sexy if their partner has just sat and

watched television while they've done all the unpleasant chores on their own!

4 Always use sex as an expression of your love and never as a weapon in a quarrel by refusing to have intercourse. If you use sex in that negative way it becomes a very destructive force.

5 If you're getting to be too busy to give each other proper love and attention, sit down with your diary and cut some things out. That applies not only to leisure activities and everyday employment but also to your Christian service. Marriage and ministry need to be balanced, and if you neglect your marriage for your ministry, then you'll end up with neither.

6 Educate yourself in the art of making love so that you know what your husband or wife finds really pleasurable. Good sexual technique is *not* sinful. People who don't take time and trouble to discover the art of foreplay and the skill of giving sexual pleasure to their partners are not being saintly, just selfish!

7 If you discover that by the time you get to bed at night you're just too tired to make love, then find a time in the day that's convenient – but make sure that you're not expecting visitors and that you've unplugged the telephone!

8 Take time to enjoy each other's company as good friends. Do lots of things together that *don't* involve sex. Couples whose only common interest is sex soon get weary of each other and grow apart.

9 Keep your relationship full of fun and laughter. Doing silly things together is almost as important in a marriage as having sex together. It keeps you young, it stops you becoming too preoccupied with responsibilities, and it makes life together much more of a joy than a duty.

10 Don't overdo it to the point where it becomes embarrassing to other people, but pay each other

compliments in company. Let everyone know that you're really glad to belong to each other. It's a good example to everyone else and it'll do wonders for your relationship.

These commandments may not have come down from the mountain carved on tablets of stone, but they are hewn out of the experience of a quarter of a century of trust, trial and tap-dancing! And talking of tap-dancing, that brings us to the next chapter ....

8 Coping with kids

MY DAUGHTER CAN TAP-DANCE!

*N*o doubt you want to know what tap-dancing has got to do with all this. So here's the explanation. Catriona, the older of our two girls, is a drama student. (She has a weakness for getting up and performing in front of an audience that I think she must have inherited from her mother!) Recently, when she came home for the Christmas holiday, she demonstrated her newly-acquired tap-dancing skills, an achievement which filled me with enormous pleasure.

It wasn't just that I've always loved the sight and sound of tap-dancing; it was more the fact that she could do it at all – considering the kind of family she comes from. I possess just enough physical co-ordination to walk, run and kick a football; and Margaret, graceful and lovely though she is, dances like someone with two left feet wearing climbing boots. But here was our daughter tap-dancing with a style and flair I could scarcely believe.

The point I'm making is this: our 'little girl' has grown into a fully independent adult with a personality and talents all of her own. That tap-dancing seemed to encapsulate for me all the wonder of being a parent, of sharing in the incredible and wonderful act of the creation of a new human being.

I couldn't help remembering the thrill of the moment when Catriona was born and I saw the funny little wrinkled creature for the first time; I couldn't help remembering all the delights and difficulties of the days when the girls were growing up; I couldn't help thinking, 'She's all my own work!' (All right, I did have a little help from Margaret!) We've said it already in this book, but we say it again – making a baby and then raising that child to independent adulthood is one of the supreme privileges and responsibilities of marriage. I'm not ashamed to say that I'm totally sold on being a dad.

But before we go on to talk about parenthood, we need to say something very important. There are, of course, couples who know the pain of childlessness. That's something for which I have a great sympathy, because we had a series of miscarriages before our daughters were born and we began to wonder if we'd ever be able to have children. Such couples need and deserve the support and understanding of family and friends. Some will be able to adopt, some will be able to conceive with medical help, but others will have to come to terms with their childlessness – never an easy thing.

Many couples respond magnificently to this disappointment and find other ways of satisfying their parental instincts by involving themselves in youth and children's work, by pouring their love on the children of friends and family, or simply by opening their hearts and their homes to those in need of friendship. They may never be parents in the conventional sense of that word, but they are often father and mother to many grateful people. Nothing that we say about parenthood should ever cause us to think of those who have been denied that privilege as being in any way 'second-class'.

WE CAN WALK THE TIGHTROPE!

Far from making us feel superior to those who have not been able to have children, becoming parents should fill us with a deep sense of gratitude for the privilege we have been given. And it should also make us very much aware of the challenge that faces us. Tap-dancing is easy compared with bringing up kids! Tap-dancers do their stuff on solid-ground, but being a parent is far more like walking a tightrope – it's a constant problem of balance. But, with practice, it can be done. And,

just so that you have a bit of help in advance, here are some of the points at which you need to watch your balance and avoid falling one way or the other.

Ideal and reality

Don't believe what glossy magazines and sentimental Mother's Day cards tell you about family life – all those images of mum, dad and two sweet and well-behaved children smiling at each other in their tidy home in which nothing is out of place. That may be the ideal, but in reality it never works like that!

The Bible tells us that God puts us in families to prevent us from being lonely (Ps 68:6a); and it's a wonderful idea. But it's also very hard work. The problem is that in a family we're all still growing and learning our roles. Parents are learning to be good parents; children are learning to be good kids while they're in the middle of the hard work of developing into young adults; none of us is an expert at our role. It's no wonder that life in a family is often tense and that there are more than a few heated exchanges. But don't despair – God still loves imperfect families.

If you don't believe me, read Genesis, the very first book in the Bible, and see what a mess some of those folk made of their families. It's all there – lying, cheating, stealing from each other, even murder – but God never gave up on them, even though the reality of family life was far from his ideal.

He'll never give up on us either. So don't imagine that your family is the only one where things go wrong. It's probably even worse in the house next door!

Give and take

A family is made up of different personalities with different points of view and different needs. So living in a family is all about give and take. There needs to be compromise and a willingness to see the other person's point of view. Parents need to remember that their kids are individuals who are entitled to their own opinions on things, and kids need to appreciate that their parents are human and that they can't be expected to be perfect all the time!

There are two sentences which need to be said and heard often in a family. One is, 'Let's talk about this'; and the other is 'I'm sorry'. If you can say those and mean them, you'll get through the most difficult situations.

Principle and prejudice

This is a difficult one – especially for parents. Distinguishing between genuine principles and personal prejudice is not easy. Let me give you an example. I loathe ear-rings and pierced ears. It seems to me that all the holes

in your body are there for a good and specific purpose, and it's beyond me why any human being should want to add an extra couple, especially in their ear-lobes! So for a long time I wouldn't allow the girls to have their ears pierced. In the end, however, having conceded that there was no principle involved, that it was just my prejudice, I gave in and allowed the deed to be done.

I still don't like the idea, but it isn't nearly so important as I was allowing it to become. Parents need to remember that fashions, hair-styles, graffiti on bedroom walls, music and such things have more to do with prejudice than principle, more to do with personal taste than absolute truth.

On the other hand, there have been occasions when I have stood firm, even when the girls didn't like me for it at the time. There are issues of honesty, chastity, and respect for authority which are not matters of personal opinion and reasonable compromise. There are times when it is right to say 'no'. The art is in knowing when.

Teaching and trusting

A good family has a minimum of rules, but that minimum must be clearly taught and lived out by the parents. And when the teaching has been done, then it is time to trust. Parents who constantly check up on their kids are actually denying them the opportunity to be free. God, our Father, has made us, his children, free to obey or disobey; and that is the only way to bring about genuine maturity.

Some years ago, we had to leave Catriona and Jenni behind for a couple of months in Bristol to complete their school-term and sit their exams after we moved to Blackpool. It was the first time they had lived apart from us. So we sat down with them both and said, 'You know what we believe, you know the standards we try to follow, you know how we want you to live. Now you have to make your own decisions. We promise you that we will not be checking up on you.'

I guess it was a risk, but love always lives with that kind of risk. Parents who don't give their kids room will either stifle them or cause them to rebel as they seek to affirm their right to make their own decisions.

Privacy and prying

Parents and kids both need space! I've learned over the years that the girls don't usually want to tell me things at the time I want to hear them. You know the kind of conversation:

> Dad: Did you have a good day at school?
> Jenni: Yeah.
> Dad: So what did you do today?
> Jenni: Oh, nothing much …

So, being a sensible and sensitive parent, I back off. But just as we're dropping off to sleep, Jenni knocks on the bedroom door and walks in saying, 'Hey, do you know what happened at school today?' And that's the time to listen.

The perfect example is the father in Jesus' story of the prodigal. The son didn't want to know his dad; he couldn't

wait to get his hands on his money so he could hit the big time. But when the money ran out and his friends ran off, he came back home to find his father waiting and ready to listen.

His father had respected the boy's freedom and now he waited to give his love and forgiveness. We must do the same. No snooping on your kids, no opening letters that arrive addressed to them and no going through their things when they're not around.

Instead, we must create the kind of atmosphere in which we're ready to listen when they need to talk.

Couples and kids

Whenever I hear parents say, 'We sacrificed everything and even neglected each other for our children,' I want to scream, 'Well, you were wrong!' Couples who live only for their kids are doing nobody a favour – least of all their kids!

We need to get this straight: marriage is the priority relationship and if it is neglected the children suffer. The quality of a marriage is absolutely vital to the overall well-being of the family. Children feel secure in a family where their parents have a loving and healthy physical relationship, where mum and dad always make time for each other, and where, without always realising it, they are absorbing a pattern for their own future marriage.

There's one more thing that needs to be said to parents on this matter of getting the balance between caring for each other and caring for the children. Don't try too hard to get on your kids' wave-length. They already have lots of friends and contemporaries, but they've only got one set of parents.

I like to think that I'm fairly 'with it' in these things, but I'm never over-impressed when I hear of parents encouraging their kids to call them by their first name. It's not so much that I'm worried about respect and that sort of thing. It's just that they've only got one mum and dad and it seems a shame to lose that relationship.

Remember that rebelling is a natural and proper part of growing up. Young people need something to kick against, just to prove to themselves that there are some definite and fixed points in life. It's part of a parent's role to be unpopular with their kids at times!

On the other hand, don't become the kind of parent who knows nothing about the world and the culture in which young people live. Some of the music your kids enjoy will sound just as strange to you as your favourite bands do to your parents. But if you keep listening you might get to enjoy it. And it'll provide you with a topic of conversation which will help keep the communication going between you.

Open and closed

This is just a word about home. Good parents encourage their kids to bring their friends home. They don't mind too much when the front room is filled with sleeping bags or when the fridge is emptied during a midnight raid. After all, it's the best way to know the kind of company your children are keeping. But don't keep such an open house that there isn't time for you to be alone as a family and to make sure you really know what is happening to each other.

Listen and lead

One of the biggest difficulties about being a parent is that over the years, without even realising it, you become so wise that you usually have the answer ready before you've heard the problem. And don't say, 'I'll never be like that' – it happens to us all when we get to be parents!

You need to learn to listen; you need to learn to 'listen between the lines', because kids don't always tell you right off what they really want to say; you need to learn to be unshockable, because your kids just won't confide in you if you gasp in horror every time they tell you what the younger generation is up to. So listen, don't jump to conclusions before you know the facts, and don't be too hasty with your answers.

But don't be afraid to balance that up by giving a clear lead. Kid's won't always like it if you tell them what they don't want to hear. But if your advice is consistent with your own life they will usually respect it and weigh it up carefully. It's never easy to know when to say 'no'. But it has to be done. Provided you do it in the right way at the right time, and provided you're not always reacting negatively, your words will be accepted.

Holy and healthy

We really covered the vital area of family devotions in the previous chapter when we emphasised the importance of making time to pray. We need to add just one or two brief observations here.

Family prayers should be both holy and healthy. They should be as natural as possible and free from the kind of stifling, artificial piety that makes kids either yawn or run for the door. It is important to have a specific time of prayer together as a family; it needn't be long – a short passage from the Bible, perhaps a comment from one of the excellent Bible reading helps which are available, and a prayer will usually be sufficient.

What is even more important is the general atmosphere

of the home. Do the members of the family love each other? Can they talk naturally about Jesus? Do their beliefs affect the way in which they live and behave towards each other? Kids need to know that their parents' Christian faith is reality rather than just religion.

Once when I was doing an interview testimony with a young woman I asked her, 'When did you first come to know Jesus?' She replied simply, 'I can't remember. He was always a part of our family.' I don't know exactly how they conducted their family prayers, but I know they must have got it dead right.

Loving and losing

There's one last bit of advice for any who want to walk the wire of parenthood. It is probably the most important of all and the most difficult to follow. You need to keep the balance between loving and losing your kids. The truth is that parents don't own their offspring! They are given to us in trust so that we can bring them up in a loving environment, teach them the truth by our words and deeds, and then send them out to make their way in the world and to create their own family.

Parental love is a love that needs to be willing to let go, to lose hold of the children so that they are truly free to grow into mature adults, able to make their own decisions and choices. Parents who are unwilling or unable to do that may think that they are protecting their children; in fact, they are stifling them and preventing them from becoming the individuals God intends them to be.

There is, of course, a wonderful bonus. Having set your

kids free, there is nothing in this world that is more fulfilling and rewarding than when they rediscover you, not just as a parent, but as a friend. That's the greatest compliment your kids can ever pay you and it makes all the hard work and all the heartache well worthwhile.

AND SO...

Having got to the end of this chapter, you might well be asking, 'Why all this stuff about bringing up kids in a book about sex?' The answer is simple and fairly obvious from the early chapters of this book: one of the main purposes of sex is to enable us to create new people and bring them up in a loving family. But today we live in a society that has separated sex from the responsibility of family life and even from the context of a loving relationship with another human being. It's time for us to move on and face that kind of thinking and to expose it for the pathetic delusion that it really is.

9 Let's fake love!

IT'S A FAKE!

Some years ago a friend of mine returned from a holiday in New York determined to impress his acquaintances with his latest purchase – a Rolex watch which he'd bought for only ten dollars from a street trader in the Big Apple! At first glance it looked impressive. There was certainly no mistaking the famous Rolex name and sign on the face of the watch.

But within a few months his bargain buy was fooling nobody. The gleaming 'gold' plate on the casing had vanished, leaving only a dull metal, the strap had broken, the glass had fallen out, and the second hand no longer worked. His 'Rolex' was, of course, a fake!

He wasn't too disappointed, however. He was smart enough to realise that you couldn't buy a high-quality watch for the money he had paid. It had given him a couple of months of use, allowed him to impress his less-sophisticated friends, and he'd lost the equivalent of only four or five pounds sterling.

Visits to various parts of the world have made me aware that there is a worldwide industry in the production and sale of fake brand-name watches and I guess the makers of the real thing must get pretty mad about people trading in on their name and reputation.

The irritation of the manufacturers of quality watches must be nothing, however, compared with the righteous anger of God at those who have taken his wonderful gift of sex and turned it into a cheap and nasty imitation. People who buy into these fake versions of sex and love stand to lose far more than a few dollars. It can cost them every scrap of decency and integrity they possess. Christian young people need to be aware of (and to beware of) the dangerous counterfeits being passed off by those who play upon the weakness and frailty of their fellow human beings.

SELFISH SEX — THE HORROR OF THE 'PORN' INDUSTRY

Pornography is one of the most insidious evils of our age. It is as well to define our terms so that we know exactly what we mean and what we are fighting against. We need to make it clear straight away that Christians are not against all sexual material in magazines and books, or in the theatre, cinema and television. If that were the case, we'd be asking for this book to be banned! There must be room for magazine articles which deal with sexual matters and problems in a helpful way, for books and videos which provide sex education for young people, and for plays and films which have genuine artistic merit and which approach sexual relationships with a sensitive presentation and a serious purpose.

We need to accept that in a society in which Christians are in a minority and in which even Christians will have different points of view, there will always be some level of disagreement as to how far writers and producers should be allowed to go in such matters, but some kind of consensus can usually be reached when there is goodwill on all sides. And we need to take the trouble to be informed so that we can participate intelligently in the debate on such matters in order that the Christian voice can be heard and that Christian values can permeate society.

The real danger, however, lies not in the realm of art and culture but in the worldwide 'porn' industry which has no moral scruples and which does not hesitate either to use the young and vulnerable in its productions or to target them with its disgusting output. Pornography refers to any material, written or audio-visual, which offends against the standards of society at large, which deals with sexual matters in a way that is designed to arouse erotic feelings, and which will – to use the legal jargon of an earlier age – tend to deprave or corrupt the individuals who read or see the material. Let's list just a few of the reasons why we find 'porn' to be so offensive.

It's an illusion

Sexual intercourse within a committed relationship is an intimate expression of love between two people who share their lives together. Sex is a part of a whole package of sharing. Pornography, on the other hand, trades in illusions. It creates an entirely false and unhealthy image of a world in which sex can be detached from everything else – from morality, from consideration for the other person, from the normal routine of life in which all sorts of other activities have to find their place. Shaw Clifton sums it up like this:

> Pornography works by hallucination. It is a cheat. The reader or watcher is intended to be sexually aroused as if he were actually experiencing the things of which he is reading or viewing. Therefore the ultimate it can bring is disappointment. It is artificial and vicarious sexual enjoyment, sex out of context, and thereby finally adds to the frustration and dissatisfaction of the one indulging in it. (*Strong Doctrine, Strong Mercy*)

It's potentially addictive

Like drugs, pornography ranges from 'soft' to 'hard', from the seemingly harmless page three nude in the daily newspaper to the appalling acts of cruelty and perversion of the video nasties which sicken even hardened members of the police force who have to look at such things in the line of duty. But even 'soft' porn is dangerous in that it promotes the belief that a woman is 'just a piece of meat for a man to jump on'.

If that seems to be stating the matter a little too forcefully, I make no apology. 'Soft' porn helps to create the kind of mental environment in which other people can be seen as nothing more than sex objects, and that is the kind of environment in which the nastier forms of porn are able to flourish.

It would be quite wrong to suggest, of course, that every user of the milder forms of pornography will inevitably progress to the really evil stuff. That would be as foolish as saying that everyone who has smoked 'pot' will become a heroin addict. But the danger of addiction and progression to more dangerous porn is, none the less, a real one.

The very fact that it deals in illusion, that it works by arousing sexual passions, means that a stronger 'fix' is needed each time as unrestrained physical appetites demand to be satisfied. Again, let's refer to Shaw Clifton's perceptive chapter on this subject. First, Shaw quotes from a letter sent by a schoolboy to Lord Longford, who published a report on pornography in Britain in the early seventies:

> Pornography is like a disease; it starts with mild forms of magazines like *Playboy* in our second and third years and ends up in our fourth and fifth years with pictures of lesbians, descriptions of sodomy etc. The result in our class is a crowd of people who want sex in any form.

Shaw then adds from his own experience of counselling those who are trapped in pornography-dependence. His words are a reminder both of the grace of God and of the fearsome nature of such addiction:

> Expert help may be required by those becoming addicted to

pornography. In some users there develops a psychological dependence on pornographic materials. I have met only two men who were addicts. Both were wretched in their self-disgust … One man was ridden with guilt, enslaved. His home was piled high with books, magazines and erotica. The road to recovery started when confession was blurted out, and the rich help and grace of God invoked. He returned home, gathered up every obscene book or paper … he had accumulated, piled it before him and then knelt in prayer: 'Lord Jesus, here are my magazines. They are filthy and abhorrent to me, yet they bind both my body and soul. You take them, please. You will know what to do with them. I want no more of them. Thank you, Lord. Amen.' Then he burned them all. Daily after that the struggle raged in him. The last time I saw him he was still victorious, daily temptation being overcome daily in Christ. I cannot report that the second man defeated his addiction. Faith, for him, was hard. (*Strong Doctrine, Strong Mercy*)

It's degrading

Pornography degrades those who produce it, those who participate in it in the case of films and videos, and those who read or watch it. In an act of sexual intercourse within a loving marriage both partners are expressing love, affection, respect and desire for each other. The very opposite is true in pornography. Human beings use other human beings as mere objects to gratify their sexual urges. Human dignity and pornography are mutually exclusive.

For the Christian who views every man, woman and child as unique and special, created by God in his own image, pornography will always be deeply offensive. Indeed, it is really a kind of blasphemy against a loving Creator. It fosters the kind of self-centred philosophy of life which leads to a loss of all values and it inevitably reaches the conclusion that a man or woman is nothing more than a bundle of powerful appetites demanding to be satisfied at all costs.

It's cruel

The dehumanising effect of pornography inevitably leads to cruelty. Don't be under any illusion on this. The glossy 'girlie' magazine is the start of a road that culminates in a dead-end of the most sickening brutality. Women and children are portrayed as disposable sex-objects who can be subjected to appalling acts of cruelty.

Let a man feed his mind on that kind of filth and it will inevitably affect his actions. I once saw a piece of graffiti which said simply, 'Pornography is the theory, rape is the practice!' Statistics and experience bear that out.

There are within each one of us primitive instincts which need to be restrained, areas of our subconscious that should not be fed and encouraged. It is to such instincts and to such areas of the human psyche that pornography appeals. It is like opening the door of the cage and allowing hungry lions to run loose among the children visiting the zoo. It can only end in trouble.

It's exploitation

There are some misguided folk who would try to defend pornography by appealing to the need for artistic freedom of expression. Don't be fooled! The purveyors of porn are motivated not by a desire to explore the human condition but to make money out of weak and vulnerable people. They are no better than the drug barons who grow rich and fat while the victims of their evil trade spend their days in a narcotic haze and die untimely deaths. Pornography is a multi-million dollar business. Behind it lies unfettered human greed.

The question is: 'What can the Christian do about it?' And to that we give four answers.

Don't touch it!

Don't touch it! Don't read the soft-porn magazines which are so freely available and which so many folk regard as a bit of harmless fun. Don't look at the kind of videos that are often passed around in schools, colleges, factories and offices. Keep away from pornography in all its forms. We are all vulnerable in the area of our sexuality, and pornographic images can light a fire in our imaginations which takes a lot of quenching.

Don't buy from those who sell it!

Don't buy from establishments that trade in pornography. If your newsagent stocks material that is questionable ask him politely to remove it and tell him that if he doesn't you'll take your custom elsewhere. If enough people hit him in his pocket he'll think twice about what he's selling.

Use your democratic muscle!

Put the pressure on the people who can change things. Raise the matter with politicians who come looking for your vote. Join one of the excellent Christian pressure groups who understand the issues and who effectively bring together Christians from all denominations to give us a stronger voice on these things.

Accentuate the positive

Demonstrate an alternative lifestyle. Too often Christians

are content just to protest against what is wrong. The world needs to see the good life in action. Let your friends and acquaintances see by the way in which you handle your sexuality and relate to the opposite sex that, far from being anti-sex, you are really positive about all that is healthy, wholesome and life-affirming.

SCI-FI SEX – THE DANGER OF THE COMPUTER AGE

There is one further word of warning that needs to be added before we can leave the subject of pornography. The appeal to the baser human instincts is being combined with the latest in computer technology. Schools are increasingly concerned about the amount of 'computer-porn' being circulated amongst young people.

Many parents are far less computer-literate than their kids and they have no idea what the piece of electronic wizardry they gave as a Christmas present is being used for. All young folk and all parents need to be on their guard against the pornography that is being made available on floppy disc or at the end of a telephone line.

But this is not the worst of it. The porn merchants have their eye on the possibilities of VR – Virtual Reality. Just in case there is anyone who doesn't yet know about VR, I'd better explain. Virtual Reality uses sophisticated computer technology to create an alternative three-dimensional world. The user wears an audio-visual helmet which provides the images and a pair of 'data gloves' which are sensitive to touch and which allow him to interact with the scene being presented to him. The technology is able to 'trick the senses' into thinking that what is going on is real.

At the time I am writing VR is still in its early stages and the best it can achieve is a cartoon-like world. But it is only a matter of time until the images become more sophisticated and more life-like, which brings us back to the sellers of porn. Through the technological magic of the computer, Virtual Reality sex is about to become a real possibility, providing the opportunity of simulated sexual intercourse with anyone in any setting you choose.

This is selfish sex taken to the ultimate limit. It takes sex out of the area of relationships and turns it into an appetite to be indulged without the unwelcome intrusion of reality. In a recent television programme the presenter described Virtual Reality sex as 'like the real thing only safer; and the machine will only ever say "no" if you want it to'.

What a prospect! It could lead to a generation of self-obsessed, self-centred people unable to handle the demands of interpersonal relationships, unable to cope with the imperfections of the real world, and unaware of the moral implications of sexual encounters.

In some form or another VR sex will soon be with us. Every concerned person should be aware of it and every Christian young person should shun it like the plague. It's a fake, albeit a very sophisticated one, and it will lead only to disappointment and disillusionment.

STUNTED SEX – THE PROBLEM OF MASTURBATION

If VR sex is the latest problem we face, masturbation must be one of the oldest. Since we've taken the trouble to define pornography and Virtual Reality, I guess we'd better define masturbation, given the possibility – admittedly a very remote one! – that someone reading this book doesn't know what the word means. Masturbation is the act of touching and manipulating your own sexual organs in order to produce an orgasm.

Of course, there are dozens of colloquial and slang words that we could use rather than 'masturbation', but since you probably know them already and since I'm not sure how to spell them, we'll leave them to your imagination! Since surveys would suggest that the great majority of single males and a large percentage of single females masturbate (not to mention the many married people who still indulge in this habit), it's unlikely that you will misunderstand what I'm talking about.

It is a practice which is surrounded by lots of old wives' tales. You must have heard them: 'Masturbation makes you deaf', or 'Masturbation affects your eyesight', or some such story. The good news is that they're all untrue. Masturbation won't do you any physical harm other than make you tired (and sore!) if you do it too often!

But masturbation is a problem, none the less, and that for two reasons. It can either make people feel terribly guilty or it can become an enslaving habit. Often both of these go together. Let's deal with the guilt thing first.

I've heard some older people tell young people that masturbation is a sin. In fact, sometimes they've seemed to suggest that it is one of the worst sins in the entire catalogue of wrongdoing. There's one problem with that argument, however, and it's this: the Bible doesn't mention masturbation anywhere. It does deal with adultery, fornication, filthy talk, incest, even bestiality – but there's not a word about masturbation.

Since the Holy Spirit managed to inspire the Bible writers to cover the subject of sin pretty fully, I can only assume that God doesn't think it helpful to label masturbation a sin. And I think God is absolutely right on this one, but then he usually is! I'll tell you why it isn't helpful to think of masturbation in terms of sin.

Our sex-drive is very powerful, especially during puberty when we are changing from being boys to men, from being girls to women. That's why sex will often figure prominently in our dreams. Often these dreams are so vivid that in the case of boys they will actually ejaculate. I believe that the technical term for such occurrences is 'nocturnal emissions', but all the people I know call them 'wet dreams'.

No-one should feel guilty about such dreams, since you haven't any control over what happens when you're asleep! They are simply the result of a build-up of sexual tension and they are nature's way of coping with this.

In the same way, because of our developing sexuality, there is a kind of inevitable 'day-dreaming' as we become aware of our sexuality and as our body prepares for full adulthood. This is what leads to masturbation, and it is far better to think of it as a part of growing up for most folk, a stage we go through rather than a sin we commit.

The problem is that it isn't always easy to leave this stage behind us. We go on 'having sex with ourselves', as masturbation has been described. Sometimes it is the case that rather than just reacting to the sexual images, thoughts and desires which inevitably come to us just because we live in a world where we are surrounded by members of the opposite sex, we move one step further and start to conjure up those images for ourselves and allow our minds to dwell on them.

That's what's happening when a boy 'mentally undresses a girl', or when someone makes use of pornography to create sexual pictures in the mind. That's where the sin part comes in. Remember when Jesus said that it is just as bad to lust after a woman as to commit adultery? That's the kind of thing he was meaning.

And the best way to deal with it is not by allowing guilt to swallow us up or by simply assuming that masturbation has to become a way of life. What we need to do is to fill our minds with other thoughts, to occupy our attention with other activities, to use our energy in other ways. You need to redirect and channel your sex drive; it's what the psychologists call 'sublimation'.

Sometimes masturbation gets a hold on people because they lack confidence in themselves and in their ability to relate to the opposite sex. So it's easier to have sex by yourself than to go through the difficult task of approaching and forming a relationship with someone. It can then develop into a vicious circle – the more inadequate you feel the more you masturbate; the more you masturbate the more inadequate you feel. And then you start to feel guilty and dirty and the whole thing goes from bad to worse.

The important thing is not to be trapped by the guilt, to realise that you're normal and special, and that God still loves you. You just need a bit of help to get over a hurdle at which many of us have stumbled.

To sum up, masturbation is really stunted sex, sex that hasn't reached maturity. It's a common part of growing up and developing into adulthood. Indeed, it often remains a part of adult life to a greater or lesser extent, particularly at times when normal sexual relations may be impossible because of illness or some other circumstance.

Even then, it is best not to think of it as sin, but more as a childish habit which has persisted into adult life – a bit like sucking your thumb or biting your nails. It isn't something God is waiting to condemn you for, but it is something you want to conquer and be free from.

If you feel that masturbation is a problem for you and that it has too strong a hold on your life, speak to a wise Christian, someone you can really trust and who will keep what you say confidential. You'll find that just talking it through helps enormously. If the person you talk to is at all sensible, he or she won't be in any way disgusted.

Masturbation is something that most of us have to deal with. And with the grace of God, some guidance and understanding from Christian teachers and leaders, and our own increasing maturity, most of us manage to deal with it and to get it under control.

10 We've messed up!

It's time to face up to the truth that there will be some
people for whom reading this book has been an
uncomfortable experience. They may well be saying
in their hearts, 'It's OK for you to write like this. But what
about me? I've already messed up. I've failed to live up to
the biblical standards. Is it too late to do anything about it?'

The answer is that it isn't too late, that God still loves
you, that there is a way forward, and that this chapter is
especially for you! What I am going to tell you may not be
easy to put into practice, but with God's help it can be

done. And in years to come you'll discover that the pain of repentance has been more than worth the effort. Here are six ABC steps to restore the health of your sexuality, and to bring it into line with God's will.

A – ACKNOWLEDGE THAT YOU HAVE FAILED TO LIVE ACCORDING TO GOD'S STANDARDS

Nothing can ever be put right until we acknowledge that something has gone wrong! Countless people have messed up their sex-lives, but they won't admit it. They find excuses, they blame other people, they point to their circumstances. But each one of us must take responsibility for our own lives and each one of us must accept that if we live outside of God's guidelines there will be trouble. That's particularly true in sexual matters. And recognising it is the first step to happiness and fulfilment in human relationships.

B – BELIEVE THAT GOD LOVES AND FORGIVES YOU – WHATEVER YOU HAVE DONE

One of the problems with sexual sin is that when it is acknowledged it can make us feel terribly guilty and dirty; it can make us feel that we are unlovable; and it can make us feel God will never want to use us again. If you are feeling like that, there are two things you need to know.

First, *God has never stopped loving you*. When we go wrong his heart is filled with pain, not disgust. There are a couple of verses in Paul's letter to the Romans which you need to hear:

> God has shown us how much he loves us – it was while we were still sinners that Christ died for us! By his sacrificial

death we are now put right with God; how much more, then, will we be saved by him from God's anger! We were God's enemies, but he made us his friends through the death of his Son (Rom 5:8-10a).

Have you got the message? God knew the worst about you and me when he sent Jesus to die for us. He didn't give his Son because we deserved it; he gave Jesus because he loves us! If he did that while our sin made us his enemies, there is no way he will turn against us now that Jesus has made us his friends!

Secondly, we cannot avoid the fact that the Bible does treat sexual sins as being very serious. It tells us that such sins are sins against our own body, which is the temple of the Holy Spirit (see 1 Cor 6:18-20). But the paradox is that Jesus never shunned people who were guilty of sexual sins.

One of the reasons the Pharisees disliked him so much was that he seemed to spend a considerable amount of his time with prostitutes, people they heartily despised. It seems that Jesus found a special joy in restoring people whose lives had been blighted by sexual sin. And he was far more condemnatory of self-righteous pride than of sexual failure.

On one occasion he was confronted with a situation in which a woman who had been caught in the very act of adultery was about to be stoned to death, a penalty the law allowed for such an offence against marriage. He turned to her accusers telling them that the one who had never sinned should throw the first stone! The missiles dropped from their hands and one by one they left the scene. Jesus tenderly assured her that he did not stand as her accuser and sent her on her way with the instruction, 'Go and sin no more.' However badly you've failed in the area of sexual conduct, you can be sure that God still loves you and longs to forgive you.

C – CONFESS YOUR SINS

When we know that God will forgive us, confession is one of the most emotionally healthy things we can ever do. As we speak out our sins to God, we experience a sense of release and cleansing. So let me suggest to you a prayer that you might use:

O God,
  I thank you that you are my Father, that you created me, and that you never stop loving me.
  I thank you for my sexuality and I accept it as a generous and special gift from you.
  I believe that you sent Jesus to die for me so that every wrong thing I have ever done can be forgiven.
  I confess to you that in my sex life I have not always lived according to your will or followed the teaching of your word.
  I particularly want to confess to you the following things in which I know I have sinned in my thoughts and in my actions … (mention specific sins of which you are aware and which are troubling you).
  I claim your forgiveness through Jesus and I ask you to fill my heart and mind with your Holy Spirit.
  Thank you, Lord. Amen.

It is also helpful to find a mature Christian, someone whom you can really trust, and to confess your sins to them. As they listen and assure you of God's love, you will discover that the sense of God's forgiveness becomes very real. It also means that in times of severe temptation – and they will definitely come to you – there will be someone

you can go to for help who knows all about you and
understands what you are facing. Do you know the song
that was popular back in the seventies? It is good advice:

> Let us open up ourselves to one another,
> Without fear of being hurt or turned away;
> For we need to confess our weaknesses,
> To be covered by our brother's love,
> To be real and learn our true identity.

You will also need to face the question as to whether you
should confess to others. I'm not suggesting, of course, that
you need to tell lots of people. That would be unwise and
unhealthy. But you must decide whether you ought to
speak to your parents, for example.

And in the case of a young person who has confessed to
God previous sexual encounters and who is now in a serious
relationship (an engagement or a friendship which is
heading in that direction), you need to seek the forgiveness
of your fiancé. It is always unwise to go into a serious
relationship with hidden secrets from the past. Skeletons
have a nasty habit of falling out of cupboards, however
firmly we think the door is locked! It's much better to clear
them out and make a fresh start with nothing to hide.

Honesty and trust are the only reliable foundations for a
lasting marriage. And certainly, if there is the slightest risk
that you might be carrying a sexually transmitted disease,
you need to make your partner aware of that fact and seek
medical advice.

D – DECIDE WHAT YOU CAN PUT RIGHT

It is a spiritual principle that true repentance must include
restitution. In other words, you not only need to put things
right with God, you need to put things right with the

people you have wronged. The story of Zacchaeus is the perfect example of restitution. After he met Jesus he promised that he would give back all the money he had acquired dishonestly. For good measure he added 300% interest!

The problem with sexual sin is that restitution is not so simple. The young man who has slept around cannot restore the virginity of the girls with whom he has had intercourse. It can be dangerous even to try to say sorry to the people we have wronged by our sexual conduct. To blunder into the life of a former girl friend who is now happily married with a young family can cause more harm than good, so you need to decide carefully what can and what cannot be put right. Sometimes there will be opportunity to make a personal apology, sometimes it will be possible to send a letter, sometimes it will be best to leave well alone. This is another area in which the wise counsel of a mature Christian will be very useful.

Of course, where a man's sexual conduct has led to the fathering of a child, it is his duty both as a Christian and as a responsible citizen to help to provide for the needs of that child until he or she reaches the age of independence.

Just in case I'm giving the impression that it is only men who need to make amends for the past, let me add that girls who have 'put themselves about' and who have put almost irresistible temptation in the way of boys also need to repent of their behaviour.

Perhaps the best way in which we can put things right is to live the kind of life that becomes an example to others, to witness to the benefits of a sex life that is in accordance with God's will, and – without parading our former sins in a way that would be sensational or that would arouse the wrong kind of interest in others – to testify to God's forgiveness and transforming power in our own experience.

E – ESTABLISH SOME BASIC RULES FOR YOUR SEXUAL BEHAVIOUR

My old dad belonged to a generation which found it too embarrassing to give advice on sexual matters. (I don't blame him too much for that. He did set me a wonderful example of how a loyal husband and father should behave.) But he did also give me one gem of wisdom and it was this: 'What you haven't had, you don't miss, but when you've gone all the way it's very difficult to stop short of that again!' I know exactly what he meant. If you've gone all the way to intercourse, it's not easy to be content with holding hands and kissing.

Here I want to give advice especially to couples who are courting, who have been having sexual intercourse, but who know that they are not living according to God's perfect will and who want to stop until they get married. It goes without saying that it isn't going to be easy to stop short of intercourse, but it can be done with discipline and with God's help.

What you need to do is to establish some rules for the way in which you're going to conduct your relationship from here on in. The first step is to make a definite act of repentance. Again the best thing is to find a mature Christian counsellor in whom you can trust, perhaps the leader of the Youth Fellowship. Talk the whole thing through with them. You'll find that will strengthen your commitment much more than simply making a private agreement with each other. Ask them to pray with you there and then and to pray for you every day. Then look again at the five rules A to E. Resolve together in the presence of God and in the presence of your counsellor that you will follow these guidelines.

Because you are human and weak there will be occasions when the temptation will be fierce. But there is a promise in the Bible that you can claim for yourself at such times:

> God keeps his promise, and he will not allow you to be tempted beyond your power to remain firm; at the time you are put to the test, he will give you the strength to endure it, and so provide you with a way out (1 Cor 10:13).

The only thing to add is that you must take the way of escape that God provides! If you hang around with temptation you're sure to lose the battle. So when temptation is really fierce, say 'Goodbye, I love you' to each other and go off and buy a hamburger, or have a shower, or play football, or stand on your head... Do anything, but get away from temptation!

My advice is similar to anyone who isn't in a serious relationship at this moment but who needs to repent of past wrong conduct. Find someone you can confide in; seek their support and prayer; resolve to follow the guidelines we've given; and when you get a new boyfriend or girlfriend begin the relationship as you mean to go on – in obedience to God's rules for safe and happy relationships.

F – FOLLOW IT THROUGH

Let me tell you about my sleek new physique! About a year ago, just after a bout of 'flu, I got on the scales and discovered to my horror that I was at least twenty pounds overweight. (I'm not the tallest of guys, so that's a fair amount!) I should have realised it – my shirt collars had been getting tighter, jogging had been getting more difficult, I'd even been having trouble with indigestion for some time – and I'd failed to heed the warnings.

Now something had to be done, so Margaret and I worked out a diet and exercise plan: no fatty foods, no big suppers late at night, no eating between meals, plenty of regular daily exercise. It was a great plan. But it needed just one more thing to be effective. We had to follow it through! I'm delighted to tell you that – with a few slips along the way – we've done just that, I've shed those twenty pounds, and I feel fitter than I have done in a long time.

But that's not all. What was at first a really difficult discipline has now become a way of life that I follow without too much thought. I developed good habits in place of the old ones, and the longer I do it the more natural it feels.

I've told you all that, not just because I like to impress my friends with my success in shedding those extra pounds, but because it's a good example of what always happens if you follow through a good resolution, and it's a good illustration of how we grow in the Christian life.

Listen to what Paul had to say to the young Christians at Colossae, many of whom had become followers of Jesus after living lives that were sexually immoral:

> You must put to death, then, the earthly desires at work in you, such as sexual immorality, indecency, lust, evil passions, and greed ... At one time you yourselves used to live

according to such desires, when your life was dominated by them. But now you must get rid of all these things … for you have taken off the old self with its habits and have put on the new self. This is the new being which God, its Creator, is constantly renewing in his own image, in order to bring you to a full knowledge of himself (Col 3:5-10).

The old way of life has to be 'put to death'. We must 'get rid of' all that belonged to it; for, as Christians, we have 'taken off the old self with its habits'. And we must 'put on the new self'; we must deliberately embrace the new lifestyle which God has planned for us, knowing that he will be constantly helping us and renewing his life in us. The demanding discipline of following his way will be transformed into the joyful experience of growing in his likeness.

AND SO...

All this is true in the area of our sexual conduct as much as in things like prayer and Bible study. God is just as concerned about our sexuality as he is about our worship and witness. When we sing, 'To be like Jesus, this hope possesses me', we are affirming the truth that the possibility of true Christian living is there even for those of us who have messed up in our sex lives! It will take effort and practice, but, as new habits replace the old ones, we will begin to experience the life and power of Jesus within us, transforming our sex lives into a pattern that will bring glory to God.

11 It's not a sin to be single!

I've never lived alone. When I left school I attended a university which was only fourteen miles or so from my home, so I continued to live with my parents. At the end of my third year I got married to Margaret and, of course, we've been together ever since. As Salvation Army officers we share our life and ministry very closely. When I'm invited to travel anywhere to speak or lecture, I accept the invitation only on the condition that it includes my wife. To be honest, I've never even cooked a meal for myself!

All of this disqualifies me from speaking with authority about being single. However, set against that, I have an enormous respect for my friends and acquaintances who live the single life. I believe that single people make an enormous contribution to the well-being of the human race, and as a married person I can point to qualities in single people which they themselves would probably be too modest to mention.

THE TYPICAL REACTION TO SINGLENESS

Let's first of all deal with a reaction to single people which is all too common. How many times have you heard a single woman described as 'an old maid'? And how often have you heard it suggested that if a man is single he must be 'queer'? Both descriptions are insulting in the way that they imply that to be single somehow or other makes you less of a person than everyone else.

In fact they're not only insulting, they're also downright stupid. People who make such remarks have obviously forgotten totally what an important part single people have always played in our society. We could make a list that would fill a book, but just think about such people as Eva Burrows, Cliff Richard, Mother Teresa, or Sir Edward Heath and the influence they have had in their different fields. You can probably add the names of dozens of single people who, though less famous, make an equally valid contribution in their own way.

It is particularly offensive for any Christian to speak disparagingly of singleness. A great company of unmarried saints and heroes, headed by Jesus himself, command our highest respect. And, of all people, those who belong to my own part of the Christian church should be first in their admiration for people who live the single life. Throughout our history and right up to the present time we owe a tremendous debt to a vast regiment of single women officers without whom the work of The Salvation Army worldwide would be drastically curtailed. William Booth was absolutely right when he said, 'Some of my best men are women!'

THE BIBLICAL POSITION ON SINGLENESS

When Paul wrote the first of his letters to the group of new Christians living in Corinth, it seems that he expected some great upheaval to take place within the lifetime of his readers. Indeed, he warns them that 'this world, as it is now, will not last much longer' (1 Cor 7:31). It is in the light of this conviction of impending trauma that he speaks to them on the subject of marriage and suggests that, 'considering the present distress' (1 Cor 7:26), it is better to stay single.

However, he is careful not to give orders on this matter because he recognises that 'each one has a special gift from God, one person this gift, another one that gift' (1 Cor 7:7). Do you realise what this means? Singleness is not a sin, it's not a sign that you're odd, it's not something to be pitied or looked down on – singleness is a gift from God!

Jesus himself says very much the same thing in Matthew's Gospel. The disciples were so taken aback by his strong teaching about the commitment required in marriage and the terrible seriousness of divorce, that they suggested to him that it might be better to remain single. Jesus gave them a very wise answer:

This teaching does not apply to everyone, but only those to whom God has given it. For there are different reasons why men cannot marry: some, because they were born that way; others, because men made them that way; and others do not marry for the sake of the Kingdom of heaven. Let him who can accept this teaching do so (Mt 19:11-12).

For most of us, God's plan is marriage and all the joy and fulfilment of a life shared with someone else. But there are some men and women whom God has called and gifted so that they are able to live the single life 'for the sake of the Kingdom of heaven'. That not only puts singleness on a high spiritual level; it also means that anyone who treats single people with anything other than respect and courtesy will have to reckon with God!

THE PRACTICAL IMPLICATIONS OF SINGLENESS

It's one thing to state the biblical principle of the importance of the single life. It's quite another thing to spell out the implications for those who have to live it out in the world of today. But we need to make that attempt if we are not to be guilty of pious platitudes. We must ask what singleness means in practical terms.

Singleness means liberty

The first thing is that singleness gives a special kind of liberty. In the section of Paul's letter to the Corinthians at which we

have already looked, the apostle puts it like this:

> I would like you to be free from worry. An unmarried man concerns himself with the Lord's work, because he is trying to

please the Lord. But a married man concerns himself with worldly matters, because he wants to please his wife; and so he is pulled in two directions. An unmarried woman or a virgin concerns herself with the Lord's work, because she wants to be dedicated both in body and spirit; but a married woman concerns herself with worldly matters, because she wants to please her husband.

I am saying this because I want to help you. I am not trying to put restrictions on you. Instead, I want you to do what is right and proper, and to give yourselves to the Lord's service without any reservation (1 Cor 7:32-35).

There is no doubt that Paul had a very high opinion of Christian marriage. (If you're in any doubt about that, read Chapter 3 again!) He saw it as a beautiful picture of the love between Christ and his church. But, equally, there is no doubt that he was also convinced that God called some to give up the privilege of marriage in order to be absolutely free to serve the wider family of all God's people.

The history of the Christian church throughout the centuries is a witness to the fact that many men and women have heeded his call to singleness in order to put themselves entirely at God's disposal. Here is the testimony of General Eva Burrows, the retired international leader of The Salvation Army:

I would naturally have very much enjoyed having children and a family. I really think that was something God required me to give up ... A single person has no-one to share with in the way that married people do. Therefore, they are thrown more on God. On the other hand, they don't have the immediate demands of family, such as the concern for children and the time that must be given to them. I don't have those kinds of demands on my time and energy. In that sense, as the apostle Paul says, I am then able to give myself entirely to the flock of God. I look upon singleness as part of my dedication to God … As soon as I entered The Salvation Army I realised that I might be called to a celibate life. I didn't rebel against it. I know that marriage is a beautiful thing, but the gift of singleness is beautiful too. God gives more than enough back to you when you give up something for him. (*General of God's Army*, Henry Gariepy)

Singleness means clarity

There is an old saying which has a lot of truth in it: 'The onlooker sees most of the game.' Often it is those people whose perspective on life is a little different from the majority of us who can see most clearly what is happening. I have certainly found this to be true in the case of  many single people I have known; the different point of view which their singleness brings, far from making them unable to deal with many of the problems of life, has actually given them a kind of clarity which is often lacking in those of us caught up in the demands of marriage and family life.

I have known unmarried social workers and school-teachers of both sexes, Roman Catholic priests and nuns, single-women Salvation Army officers and a host of other single people who have brought unique insights to the vital tasks in which they were engaged. I know that whenever I have to form a committee to deal with some thorny problem or a 'think-tank' to work through and plan an event, I always want to have a good proportion of single people as part of the group.

Interestingly, the insight of single people is often particularly useful when applied to the problems of marriage. What they lack in personal experience of married life, they more than make up for by their ability to take a detached and objective look at the issues involved. It was C. S. Lewis, one of the finest thinkers of the twentieth century, who said that he didn't like jokes about single women since some of the best minds he had ever encountered had inhabited the bodies of so-called 'old maids'.

Singleness means responsibility

When I was a kid I had an auntie who was an extremely practical person. So every Christmas, instead of toys and sweets, she gave me clothes – hand-knitted pullovers and other such  'useful' things. The only problem was that, as a typical ten-year-old boy, I didn't want that kind of gift; I much preferred the toys and sweets!

I have a hunch that some readers – especially some of the single ones – will be feeling exactly the same regarding all this talk about singleness as a gift. You're probably thinking to yourself, 'This isn't a gift I want! I want a partner, a satisfying sexual relationship, a home and children.'

In one sense, since I'm not a single person and don't have to live with the demands of the single life, I've no right to say anything to you. On the other hand, just as single people can bring a sense of perspective to the problems of married people, maybe I can be of some help on this one. At least I'm going to try, and I hope this is helpful.

There is no way you can escape the fact that singleness does bring a very heavy responsibility. For the Christian singleness means celibacy — abstinence from sexual relations – and that isn't easy in the kind of world we live in. Some people try to cope with this by suppressing their sexual feelings, pretending they don't exist. It hardly needs to be said that that is both wrong and dangerous; it's like trying to hold the lid down on a steaming kettle – one way or another the steam will get out. Suppression can lead only to bitterness or sexual perversion, and God does not want any of us to take those routes.

Happily, there are other ways to go. First of all, you need to accept your sexuality and to acknowlege that your strong hunger for a sexual relationship and your deep desire for children and family are perfectly normal. That is how God made you and you cannot and must not be ashamed of it.

When the pressure is great you need to find a good and trusted friend with whom you can talk the whole thing through; that is one of the ways in which 'the lid of the kettle' can be gently lifted and the steam allowed to escape. And always you need to find ways to direct and channel your sexuality and energy into positive avenues that bring fulfilment to you and benefit to others.

What we must never forget, whether we are male or female, is that it is our sexuality which makes us able to be tender, loving and sensitive people. Take that away from us and we cease to be fully human. When our sexuality cannot find fulfilment in the act of intercourse between a man and a woman, it can find a different kind of fulfilment in loving, caring service. That is not to say that the struggle against temptation will always be easy, but it does mean that it can have positive and healthy results.

There are just two more things I want to say on this subject. The first is that God is full of surprises and sometimes he decides that it's time for us to have an entirely different gift. (I wish my auntie had been able to do the same when I was a kid!) If you're single and you want to be married, don't give up hope.

One of our closest friends was single until her mid-forties. She was independent, talented, self-sufficient and entirely at ease with herself as a single person. Then she fell head over heels in love with a man who felt the same way about her. I conducted their wedding a few years ago and it was one of the happiest tasks I've ever performed. They visited us recently and they're as crazy about each other as any young lovers.

Their story is not unique. I've known folk get married for the first time in their sixties and find real happiness and satisfaction in their new relationship. It isn't wrong to keep hoping and to ask God that he might consider swapping the gift he's given you for something more suitable!

And that brings me to my last words on singleness; you need to trust your sexuality and your future to God. If, as Christians believe, God really did become fully human in Jesus, then he knows all about the single life with its wonderful potential for fulfilment and service. He also knows all about sexual frustration and temptation, he knows all about loneliness, and he knows all about the longing for a partner and for family.

AND SO...

Whether you are the kind of person who feels totally comfortable about being single, or whether you are struggling with your situation, God understands and supports you. Let's close this chapter with a prayer which might provide you with a pattern on which to base your own prayers:

Dear God,

I know that you created me, that you love me and that you understand me fully.

I thank you that my sexuality is good and is all part of being made in your image.

I thank you for the life and example of Jesus who lived the single life, who delighted in the company of men and women and children, who blessed the marriages of others without resentment, and reached out in forgiveness and healing to those whose sex lives were damaged by sin. If it is your will that I should remain single, I thank you for the freedom my singleness gives me. Help me always to be positive about my sexuality and to channel it in ways that are healthy, life-affirming and beneficial to others.

If it is your will that I should get married and enjoy the privilege of family life, I ask you to lead me to the right person with whom I can share my life and serve you faithfully.

I trust my life, my sexuality and my future to your loving care. Amen.

12 But what if I'm gay?

*T*here's no doubt that there is a significant minority of people who are strongly attracted to members of the same sex rather than those of the opposite sex. Just how large a percentage of the population is homosexual is a matter for debate. The gay lobby would put the figure at somewhere around ten per cent, but increasingly the objectivity of their research and the accuracy of their statistics are being called into question. Recent surveys would suggest that a figure of three per cent is much nearer the truth.

If that is the case – assuming, of course, that fifty people have read this book! – then at least one or two readers have got to be saying, 'But what about me? I think I'm gay,' or 'What have you got to say to me? I know I'm a lesbian.' If you're asking those kind of questions, then this chapter is especially for you.

But before everyone else decides to skip the next few pages, I want you to know that it's also for *you*. Homosexual people have suffered a great deal of unkindness from their heterosexual brothers and sisters who have often refused to take the time and trouble to discover the facts about homosexuality and who have often been guilty of sheer prejudice and even hatred.

I'm ashamed to admit it, but sometimes Christians have been as guilty as anyone of failing to love and accept those whose sexuality is different from their own. I've heard Christians use words like 'dike' or 'poof' – and worse – far too often for comfort.

The teaching of Jesus would strongly suggest that God will judge our lack of love with far greater severity than the sexual frailties of those we are often tempted to despise. So make sure you stay with this chapter. It'll definitely have something to say to you!

The best way we can approach this subject in a fairly short chapter is by asking simple questions which demand a direct answer. Those answers will be brief; but they will, I hope, point you in the right direction as you continue to think and pray about this matter.

WHAT MAKES YOU THINK THAT YOU'RE HOMOSEXUAL?

That may sound like a silly question with an answer that's all too obvious, but it really is a question you need to

ask yourself if you think you're homosexual. The truth is that many young people go through a phase in which they are confused about their sexuality. Girls, for example, often feel a strong attraction to an older woman, perhaps a teacher. And many boys go through a stage in which they will participate in mutual masturbation with other young males.

It's too easy to conclude from such experiences that you must be homosexual. But that is not necessarily the case. This is what two psychologists have to say on the matter:

Perhaps 20% or more of young people have one or more homosexual experience during their late childhood or early adolescent years. Thus homosexual contacts seem to be somewhat more common than true homosexual preferences, in which only persons of the same sex are seen as possible affectional partners. Indeed, it has been suggested that homosexual contacts among both adolescent boys and girls are quite common but have no lasting implications for normal sexual development. In fact, we might think of typical same-sex contacts in the early adolescence as mutual masturbation rather than as the acting out of a true homosexual preference. In other words, boys, or girls, as couples are involved in exploring sexual feelings rather than expressing their attraction to one another. A difficulty often arises, however: adolescents themselves assume that because they found such experiences pleasurable, they may be homosexuals. As in many other instances, how we label or explain our experiences is often more important than the experiences themselves. (*Adolescent Psychology*, Norman A. Sprinthall & W. Andrew Collins, Random House, New York, 1984)

The message is simple: don't assume that you're gay or lesbian because of one or two sexual experiences with members of the same sex. It may simply be a part of your growing up. It's too easy, especially if you find it difficult to establish relationships with the opposite sex, to conclude that you are definitely homosexual. Your sexuality is far too important for you to make a snap judgement based on a few adolescent encounters.

It's also important to add that none of us is 100% heterosexual in the sense that it would be impossible for us ever to feel any kind of sexual stimulation in the presence of a member of the same sex. For example, during wartime when many men were separated not only from their wives but from contact with any females, there is no doubt that a certain number of homosexual contacts took place between men who were otherwise heterosexual. But, when circumstances returned to normal, those men reverted to heterosexual behaviour.

WHAT MAKES SOME PEOPLE HOMOSEXUAL?

Having given the warning that no-one should assume they are homosexual without a great deal of thought, we need, none the less, to accept the fact that for many people their sexual attraction to members of the same sex is something far deeper than a passing phase. Why should that be? What makes some people homosexual?

The short answer to this question is that we don't really know. It has sometimes been suggested that homosexuality is an inherited condition. But there is little evidence to back up the theory that heredity is the primary cause. Some research has been done into genetic factors such as the presence of abnormal levels of certain hormones. But no definite conclusions have been reached.

On a much cruder level, the popular view of the

homosexual is that of the 'butch' lesbian or the effeminate male. But neither of these pictures matches up to the facts. Homosexual people seem to be as different as heterosexuals in their physical make-up and their personality.

It seems likely that environment and up-bringing are far more significant than genetic factors in this matter. One writer I read expressed it in computer jargon by saying that we are born 'wired for sex, but not programmed'. To put it another way, we are sexual creatures with strong sexual appetites; that is a  'given' in all of us. But how our sexuality is expressed and who or what becomes the object of our desire is largely conditioned by the impact of the world around us.

Sometimes psychologists speak of 'push' and 'pull' factors with regard to homosexuality. 'Push' factors prevent the development of heterosexual behaviour and can include such things as a pathological fear of venereal disease, a sense of disgust at the thought of the sex organs of the opposite sex, or a general feeling of resentment against members of the opposite sex. 'Pull' factors draw a person towards homosexuality and can include the need to compensate for a sense of inadequacy in relationships with the opposite sex, or the need for a strong emotional relationship with an older person of the same sex.

There is a strong body of opinion that one of the major pressures which predisposes a person towards homosexuality is the presence of difficulties in the parent-child relationship. Case studies of male homosexuals often reveal that the father has been absent from the family home for prolonged periods, that he has been weak in his fulfilment of his male role in the family, or that he has been actively hostile towards his son, constantly criticising him and putting him down. The lack of a role model – someone who reinforces and clarifies male heterosexual behaviour, someone to be admired and imitated – seems to be a major factor in predisposing young men to homosexuality.

We are not, of course, suggesting that all parents of homosexual children have wilfully neglected their role. That clearly is not the case and it would be cruel to suggest that it was. But somehow, somewhere along the way, something does seem to have gone wrong in the relationship. Dr Elizabeth Moberly sums it up like this:

> A homosexual orientation depends ... on difficulties in the parent-child relationship, especially in the earlier years of life ... Amidst a welter of details, one constant underlying principle suggests itself: that the homosexual has suffered from some deficit in the relationship with the parent of the same sex. (*Homosexuality: A New Christian Ethic*, Dr Elizabeth Moberly, James Clarke, Cambridge, 1983)

Perhaps the only sure answer to the question, 'What makes people homosexual?' is that it is one of the consequences of living in a fallen world. The teaching of the Bible is that God created human beings in his own image to enjoy perfect fellowship with him. We, however, have abused the freedom that he has given us and we have chosen to follow our own way rather than God's.

Our sinfulness has affected every part of creation and every aspect of our lives. Things are not as they should be. Where there should be peace there is war, where there should be goodness there is sin, where there should be health there is sickness, where there should be happy integrated personalities there is unhappiness and inner disharmony. Homosexuality is part of that imperfection which has spoiled and marred God's world and our lives. We all have personalities that are flawed by sin, we all carry our areas of weakness. Homosexuality is simply one of those human frailties with which some people have to cope.

WHAT DOES THE BIBLE HAVE TO SAY ABOUT HOMOSEXUALITY?

There are many people today, including some Christians, who argue that homosexual relationships are just as good and just as valid as heterosexual relationships, provided that the two people involved love and respect each other. That *seems* a reasonable and tolerant position, but before we accept such a judgement we need to ask what God thinks about homosexual relationships. What we actually discover when we turn to the Bible is that homosexual activity is unequivocally condemned in five different places.

In Leviticus 18:22 we are told that 'No man is to have sexual relations with another man; God hates that.' And a little later in the same book the death penalty is actually laid down for such acts (Lev 20:13). The writers of the Old Testament were clearly convinced that God has ordained sexuality as an expression of love between the sexes, as a powerful force for the creation of new people, and that he has strictly forbidden sexual relationships between people of the same sex.

Obviously, we are not suggesting that God wants homosexuals put to death today! We live in the new dispensation in which he offers love and forgiveness to all men and women through Jesus. But we cannot avoid the conclusion that God sees widespread homosexual practice as a serious threat to the health and stability of society.

The New Testament is equally emphatic in its insistence that homosexual acts are outside of God's plan for humanity. In the first chapter of the letter to the Romans, Paul writes about the fact that the human race has turned away from God and has substituted other things in his place. The outcome of this is that, having abandoned the truth about God, our minds are filled with confusion and we are at the mercy of our sinful desires. One of the results of this sad state of affairs, according to Paul, is the widespread occurrence of homosexual activity:

> God has given them over to shameful passions. Even the women pervert the natural use of their sex by unnatural acts. In the same way the men give up natural sexual relations with women and burn with passion for each other. Men do shameful things with each other, and as a result they bring upon themselves the punishment they deserve for their wrongdoings (Rom 1:26-27).

It is significant that in this passage homosexual acts are described as 'unnatural'. Some people argue that this cannot apply to homosexuals who have always felt attracted to members of the same sex: for them homosexual acts feel completely 'natural'. But 'natural' here does not refer just to individual feelings but what is 'natural', i.e. 'according to nature' as God intended.

I once got so angry with a drunk who shouted obscenities at me that the most 'natural' thing in the world was for me to punch him hard on the nose! But however natural it felt to me at the time, it clearly wasn't the kind of behaviour God intended for me! In the same way, however 'natural' a homosexual relationship might feel to the people involved in it, it is not according to God's will and plan.

There are two more New Testament passages which clearly forbid homosexual conduct. One is in the first letter to the Corinthians where Paul includes practising homosexuals in a list of wrongdoers who will not possess God's Kingdom (1 Cor 6:9-10). The reasoning behind his statement is obvious. The Kingdom of God is the realm in which his will is done and his commandments obeyed. Anyone, therefore, who persists in following a lifestyle opposed to God's revealed will excludes himself from God's Kingdom.

The final reference is found in the first letter to Timothy. The writer's argument here is simply that the law exists to control those who actions are 'contrary to sound doctrine' (1 Tim 1:8-11) – in other words, those who do not follow the teaching of Scripture. Homosexuals are included in the list of wrongdoers who merit the censure of the law.

There is no room for doubt that a homosexual lifestyle is incompatible with the plain teaching of the Bible. Indeed, there are a number of other passages in which the sinful nature of such activity is clearly implied (e.g. Gen 14:4-9; Judg 19:22-26; 2 Pet 2:1-22; Jude 7). So the Christian who is aware of strong homosexual desires must face up to the crunch question, 'What am I going to do about this?'

SO WHAT CAN I DO IF I'M GAY?

As with most situations in life, homosexuality presents us with an array of alternatives. Before we look at those alternatives, we must make one thing clear: no-one should be condemned for their sexual orientation. It is not a sin to feel attracted to members of the same sex. It is how we react to those feelings which matters.

The Bible does not condemn homosexual people. But it does strongly condemn homosexual activity. None of us, homosexual or heterosexual, can completely avoid temptation. But every one of us is responsible before God for the choices we make and for the way in which we respond to temptation.

Get into the gay scene?

The most obvious course of action for the person who believes they are gay is to get into the gay/lesbian scene, to accept and openly declare their homosexuality and to embark upon a homosexual relationship. All that we have said thus far in this chapter will have made it clear that that is not an option for the Christian who wants to take the teaching of the Bible seriously.

Get tough?

Is the only alternative, then, to get tough, to develop an iron will, to accept a regime of rigid sexual self-discipline which says 'no' to all sexual desire and temptation? At first glance there is something to be said for this course of action. All of us, whether homosexual or heterosexual, have to exercise discipline in the area of our sexuality. If we gave in to ourselves every time we were sexually attracted to someone the consequences would be disastrous!

But tough discipline by itself is not sufficient. I know enough people who've tried to handle things in this way to be able to tell you that it's like trying to keep the lid on a boiling saucepan; one way or another the steam has to escape and any attempt to contain it will result ultimately in an explosion. Sheer will-power is not enough to control our sexual desires. Sooner or later they will demand satisfaction.

Get busy?

The same objections can be made to the advice that the homosexual should get busy. Whilst it's true that an active life – especially one that makes time to care for others, thinking of their problems rather than concentrating on our own – channels a great deal of energy that would otherwise be directed toward a sexual object, it's equally undeniable that busy-ness is no escape from our sexuality. Indeed, the very activity in which we are engaged can often lead us into situations where the pressure of temptation is almost overwhelming.

Get treatment?

Homosexuality is an illness, some claim, so the answer is to get treatment. Again there may be a certain element of truth in this suggestion. Certainly, skilled counselling from psychologists and psychiatrists is of help to many homosexual people dealing with the problems of depression and loneliness which are often linked with their sexual orientation. And there is a psychological technique known as 'desensitisation' which has apparently had some degree of success in diminishing the strength of unwanted sexual urges. Moreover, there are some forms of psychoanalysis which have been used to redirect the sexual orientation of homosexual people.

None of these approaches, however, has been an unqualified success. In addition, it is highly questionable whether it is right or helpful to think of homosexuality as an illness. Such an approach has a number of serious consequences: it takes away the individual's personal responsibility for dealing with their sexuality, it tends to separate homosexuals from heterosexual society and allows prejudiced people to dismiss them as freaks to be pitied or shunned, and it suggests that there is a simple 'cure' for homosexuality; this is rarely the case and the absence of such an immediate remedy can often serve to deepen the homosexual's sense of isolation.

Get married?

I've frequently heard it said that the way to be free from homosexuality is to get married. The love and company of a good spouse, the argument runs, will soon redirect a person's sexual orientation.

Of all the advice that can be given to a homosexual, this is probably the most stupid and most dangerous! Not only does it involve an evasion rather than a resolution of the problem, but it also means that the lives of two people can be made desperately unhappy.

Sexual problems do not disappear when we get married. Too many gay men and lesbian women have tried to deal with their homosexuality in this way only to discover that their sexuality remains unchanged and that their marriage eventually ends in disaster.

Get grace

That leaves us with only one way for the homosexual who wants to be obedient to God's will: that is to get grace – to seek the love and forgiveness and support of God himself. The struggle will not be easy, but there is hope. God loves us whatever our sexual orientation at this moment, and he longs that we should be free to be all he wants us to be.

We referred earlier to the passage in 1 Corinthians 6, in which Paul includes practising homosexuals in the list of wrongdoers who will not possess God's Kingdom. It's now time to quote that passage because it ends, not with condemnation, but with a message of hope for all:

> Surely you know that the wicked will not possess God's Kingdom. Do not fool yourselves, people who are immoral or who worship idols or are adulterers or homosexual perverts or who steal or are greedy or are drunkards or who slander others or are thieves – none of these will possess God's Kingdom. Some of you were like that. But you have been purified from sin; you have been dedicated to God; you have been put right with God by the Lord Jesus Christ and by the Spirit of our God (1 Cor 6:9-11).

What a wonderful message for homosexuals and heterosexuals alike. We are all sinners in need of God's forgiveness and transforming power: 'Some of you were like that. But you have been purified from sin...' God transformed the members of the church at Corinth in the first century and he can change us in the twentieth century, whatever our weakness! So let's try to give some specific advice as to how the homosexual can put himself or herself in the place where God's grace can reach and begin to change their lives.

GETTING GRACE

Acknowledge who and what you are

You are a person of worth, created in the image of God. And, like every other human being, you are a sinner with particular weaknesses and temptations. The baggage you carry through life happens to include a homosexual orientation and that is something which by God's grace you need to overcome. Remember that in God's eyes you are no worse and no better than any other sinner.

Ask God for his forgiveness and help

God does not want anything to separate you from his love. If you have been involved in homosexual activities which fall under the condemnation of the Bible, ask God to forgive you. And ask him to fill your life with his Holy Spirit to enable you to resist temptation.

Begin to develop new thought-patterns and new habits

There is no 'quick fix' for deep-seated patterns of behaviour. It takes time to change your lifestyle. But you do have to make a definite start. If you have been reading the kind of books or watching the kind of films which encourage a gay lifestyle, give them up. If you have been attending the kind of clubs which put you in the way of temptation, stop going to them. Then make sure that you fill the vacuum that is left. Read different books, join new clubs, find new friends, take up new activities.

Get a group of Christian people to support and pray for you

One of our problems today is that we have become too individualistic. God never intended that we should fight every battle on our own. The Christian church is the community of God's people within

which we ought to be able to find support and help.

The love of God means that there is hope for every individual and for every human condition. The homosexual must not accept his or her situation as being beyond God's transforming power and grace. Some will testify that God has removed all desire for same-sex relationships and that they have found fulfilment in heterosexual marriage. Others will acknowledge that their homosexual orientation is still very much present but that God gives them grace to resist temptation and to channel their energies in a positive way.

And the rest of us must not fail to be God's people, the body of Christ on earth, accepting all kinds of sinners, and sharing the grace of God through our love. Our care for our homosexual brothers and sisters should be all the greater as we begin to understand the struggles they face and the support they need. Together we can demonstrate a new way of life to a world in which sexuality is just one more casualty of human sin and selfishness.

13 Let the revolution begin!

As I was getting ready to write this final chapter in the middle of June 1994, I came across a brief report in one of the UK's popular tabloid newspapers which immediately grabbed my attention. It announced that a new sexual revolution is turning the heads of America's youth and that many adolescents are shunning the sexual promiscuity initiated by their parents' generation in favour of self-imposed celibacy. According to the report, more than 200,000 young people have 'taken the pledge to remain celibate until they are married' under the banner of the *Love Can Wait* organisation.

I was so delighted by this good news that I actually shouted 'Yee-haw' in my best American accent! Revolutions happen when people become unhappy with the *status quo* and begin to long for change. All it needs is for one or two people to take the lead and others are sure to follow. All power to everyone involved in the *Love Can Wait* movement. This is the kind of sexual revolution we need. It's got to be good.

Of course, we don't all live in America with its strong church-going constituency which provides a basis for such a movement. Those of us who live in other parts of the world, where the Christian church is not as large in numbers and where sexual attitudes have moved a long way from Christian standards, may well be tempted to feel that it's too late for the tide to turn; that society is too far gone to change. But I don't believe that that is the case.

I'm old enough to remember when everyone thought that we should drink gallons of full-cream milk and that fatty foods were good for you! But as people have learned the facts and become much more health-conscious they have demanded change. Low-fat foods and fat-free diets are now the order of the day. I can also recall the days when the majority of the population smoked and when it was considered antisocial to object to anyone smoking. Again, as the truth about the effects of tobacco have become known, more and more people have given up the habit and more and more businesses and other organisations are prohibiting smoking on their premises. When the truth gets out attitudes can and do change.

In an age which has seen a widespread increase in divorce and in the break-up of families, and in which the appearance of the AIDS epidemic has demonstrated the terrible consequences of a promiscuous lifestyle, the time is right for 'a new sexual revolution', as the newspaper article describes it. Anyone with any common sense can see the mess society is in; and if we can succeed in telling them the truth about sex as God intended it to be, the clamour for revolution might well become irresistible.

The question is, 'Are *you* prepared to be a leader in the sexual revolution?' No, I haven't made a mistake. I don't mean simply 'Are you prepared to *join* the revolution?'; I really do mean that the leadership depends on *you*! I'm assuming that most of you reading this book are young people, and it's your generation that will need to change the world. My generation is the one that has failed in the area of sex, the one that has sold God's great gift for what it thought was sexual freedom.

In fact, the deal turned out to be one of the worst bargains ever made. Our so-called freedom has proved to be nothing more than a cleverly disguised slavery to selfishness and second-rate thrills. People like me can support, advise and encourage you, but you're the ones who need to go for it! So here, by way of support, encouragement and advice, are my three rules for leaders of the sexual revolution.

TELL IT LIKE IT REALLY IS!

One of the greatest difficulties you will face is that this is an age of moral relativism. The great majority of people don't really believe in objective truth and definite standards any longer. One man's version of the truth is as good as the next man's, and nobody knows where to find a morality which is bigger than the individual and which applies to everyone. You can believe anything you like as long as you don't believe it too strongly!

Christians see things very differently. We believe that God has revealed his character and his will for us in his written Word. In the matter of sex, as in everything else, we take our standards from the Bible. So, if we are to tell it as it really is, we need to *be biblical*. We need to know what the Bible teaches, we need to base our own conduct on what the Bible teaches, and we need to tell others what the Bible teaches. I hope that this little book will have helped you to be clearer on the biblical view of sex.

I'm not suggesting, of course, that when you are speaking to non-Christians you should just quote them great chunks of the Bible. That wouldn't carry any weight with them and might well cause them to switch off from what you're saying. But in discussions on sex your stance will always be the biblical one, and you will try to explain that you accept biblical teaching not just 'because God says so', but because you've proved that it makes more sense than anything else and that it actually works better than anything else.

That means that you'll sometimes have to take a stand that will be unpopular. The usual line on sex today is, 'You can do whatever turns you on, provided you try not to hurt others too much.' But Christians believe that some things are wrong in God's eyes, whether or not they turn you on. So as well as being biblical, you will need to *be bold*. It may lose you a few friends in the short term, but in the long term people always respect someone who stands firm for their convictions.

It goes without saying that you need to make your case with courtesy and that you need to be willing to listen to other points of view, even when you believe them to be wrong. Heated arguments rarely result in anyone being persuaded. You will often need to state the Christian position gently and leave it at that. Don't worry if you don't seem to have convinced everybody. God will honour your words and your sincerity.

LIVE IT LIKE GOD REALLY INTENDED!

Be holy!

Someone once said about a Christian whose lifestyle didn't match up to his words, 'I can't hear what he is saying because his actions shout too loud'! If you are going to take your part in leading a sexual revolution, your deeds will be even more important than your words, and what you *are* will matter more than what you *say*. You have to live your life before the critical gaze of a watching world, so you must be holy in all your conduct.

Some Christians have somehow or other got hold of the idea that holiness is something for a select few Christians and that it doesn't have a lot to do with the nitty-gritty of ordinary life. But they're dead wrong! It's highly significant that in one of the earliest references to the holy life in the New Testament, Paul addresses new Christians on one of the key areas to which holiness applies – their sexual conduct:

> For you know the instructions we gave you by the authority of the Lord Jesus. God wants you to be holy and completely free from sexual immorality. Each of you men should know how to live with his wife in a holy and honourable way, not with a lustful desire, like the heathen who do not know God. In this matter, then, no man should do wrong to his fellow-Christian or take advantage of him. We have told you this before, and we strongly warned you that the Lord will punish those who do that. God did not call us to live in immorality,

but in holiness. So, then, whoever rejects this teaching is not rejecting man, but God who gives you his Holy Spirit (1 Thess 4:2-8).

Holiness is not an optional extra; it is not something to be turned on every Sunday; it is not something which applies only to the 'religious' part of our lives. It is the life and love of Jesus in us and it has to be demonstrated in every area of life, not least in our sexual conduct. We don't just preach against adultery, sexual promiscuity, and pornography. We show positively by our lifestyle that God can set us free from slavery to our sexual impulses, free to live a life of loyalty to our husband or wife, free to be holy and Christlike in the most basic aspects of our humanity.

Be healthy!

But let me add one word of caution; holiness is a long way from prudishness! Genuine holiness is the most attractive thing in the world; pious prudishness sends normal red-

blooded human beings running in the opposite direction! I hope that this book has made it clear that Christians are entirely positive about sex. We're not embarrassed about it and we're not ashamed of our sexuality. We simply believe that such a wonderful gift has got to be used according to the instructions of the God who invented it and gave it to us.

So don't just be holy in your conduct; be healthy in your attitude. Christians will never participate in any talk that is smutty or suggestive. But Christians do have a healthy sense of humour. There is a right time and a right way to laugh about sex as we do about every other aspect of human behaviour.

I will never forget being in a meeting in which a preacher with a rather florid style of delivery told us that he had attended a conference where everything was perfect – the weather, the food, the seminars, the accommodation – everything. Then, just to put the final touch to his glowing description of the event, he added, 'And between sessions, we all went into the garden and had intercourse.' He was using the word 'intercourse' in its dictionary sense of 'any social communication between human beings'. But the congregation understood the word in its more normal usage, and the result was a roar of uncontrollable laughter.

I don't believe for a minute that we would have been more holy if we hadn't laughed. In fact, I don't think we would have been *human* if we hadn't been highly amused! And it wouldn't surprise me in the least to discover that there was laughter in heaven at that moment. God wants us to be holy *and* healthy when it comes to sex.

FACE UP TO WHERE IT'S REALLY AT!

Be aware!

Too often Christians are guilty of hiding away in their respectable religious ghettos and ignoring what's going on outside or being so shocked by it all that they don't know what to do. That's a luxury we can't afford if we are going

to start a sexual revolution. We need to face up to where it's really at.

In short, we must be aware of what is happening in the world around us. People's moral standards and sexual habits have changed enormously in the last twenty years and it's no use us pretending otherwise. The advent of much-easier birth control, the widespread rejection of Christian values, the breakdown of traditional forms of marriage and family life have all brought about a whole new way of thinking about sex and a whole new way of behaving.

We need to watch what's on television, read what's in our newspapers, and listen to the lyrics of the latest song that's topping the charts, if we want to know where our non-Christian neighbours are finding their standards for the way they live. When we want to tell them about Christian values, we need to be able to start from where they are in order to lead them to where they should be.

We need to pray especially for those Christians who work in politics, in the media, in education, in the world of entertainment, and in any other sphere of life where they have an opportunity to influence opinion in a very powerful way. And we need Christians in every walk of life who dress like everyone else around them, who look like everyone else around them, who speak like everyone else around them, but who have a lifestyle that is radically different because it is based on God's standards as they are laid down in the Bible.

Our non-Christian friends should find us the most normal and sane people in the world; and yet, at the same time, they should know there is an uncompromising difference in us which raises in them a longing to find the purpose and pattern for life that we have found. A happy Christian marriage says more to the world about God's will for our sex lives than a dozen speeches; a young person who can talk about the latest trends in music and fashion but who upholds Christian standards in his or her relationships with the opposite sex will be a more effective witness than almost anything else you can think of.

Be alert!

But one last word before I close. If you make it *your* business to stand for truth and righteousness, the devil will make it *his* business to try to trap you in temptation. That is especially the case in  the area of sex where we are all very vulnerable. So be alert! Heed the advice we've tried to give in this book about keeping away from temptation. Take time to pray and make sure that you have asked some Christian friends to pray for you as well.

Being at the forefront of a revolution is never easy, but here is the best encouragement I can give you. Jesus himself is praying for you at every moment; we are promised that in Hebrews 7:25. And if you want to know the kind of prayer he is making to his Father, then check out the prayer he made for all his disciples in every age on the night before he was arrested:

> I do not ask you to take them out of the world, but I do ask you to keep them safe from the Evil One ... I sent them into the world just as you sent me into the world. And for their sake I

dedicate myself to you, in order that they, too, may be truly dedicated to you ... I made you known to them, and I will continue to do so, in order that the love you have for me may be in them, and so that I also may be in them (Jn 17:15, 18-19, 26).

With that prayer for God's protection and that promise of the presence of Jesus within us, we can confidently challenge the world by our words and actions to discover the true joy and purpose of God's gift of sex. Let the sexual revolution begin!

APPENDIX

The Marriage Ceremony

1. As the bride and bridegroom stand forward, the officiating officer shall say to the congregation:

We are gathered here in the sight of God, and in the name of the Lord Jesus Christ, to join this man and this woman in holy matrimony which has been sanctioned and blessed by Jesus Christ, and declared in Scripture to be honourable among all men.

2. The officiating officer shall then say to the bride and bridegroom:

I exhort you both to enter into this new and holy relationship with reverent thought, honest intention, and in the fear of God, duly considering the purpose for which marriage has been ordained.
    I require and charge you both in the presence of God and of this congregation that if either of you knows anything to prevent you from being lawfully married you do now declare it.

3. The bridegroom shall then say after the officiating officer, using all names:

I DO SOLEMNLY DECLARE THAT I KNOW NOT OF ANY LAWFUL IMPEDIMENT WHY I, ... MAY NOT BE JOINED IN MATRIMONY TO ...

4. The bride shall then say after the officiating officer, using all names:

> *I DO SOLEMNLY DECLARE THAT I KNOW NOT OF ANY LAWFUL IMPEDIMENT WHY I, … MAY NOT BE JOINED IN MATRIMONY TO …*

5. The officiating officer shall then ask the bridegroom:

> *…, will you take … to be your wife, to live according to God's ordinance in holy matrimony? Will you love her, comfort, honour and sustain her, and, forsaking all others, be faithful to her as long as you both shall live?*

6. The bridegroom shall answer:

> *I will.*

7. The officiating officer shall then ask the bride:

> *…, will you take … to be your husband, to live according to God's ordinance in holy matrimony? Will you love him, comfort, honour and sustain him, and, forsaking all others, be faithful to him as long as you both shall live?*

8. The bride shall answer:

> *I will.*

9. The bridegroom shall then take the bride's right hand in his and say after the officiating officer:

> *I CALL UPON THESE PERSONS HERE PRESENT TO WITNESS THAT I, …, DO TAKE THEE, …, TO BE MY LAWFUL WEDDED WIFE, to have and to hold from this day forward, for better for worse, for richer for poorer, in sickness and in health, to love and to cherish, till death us do part, according to God's*

holy ordinance; and this I declare upon my honour (Salvationists add:) *as a true soldier of Jesus Christ.*

10. They loose hands, and then the bride shall take the bridegroom's right hand in hers and say:

I CALL UPON THESE PERSONS HERE PRESENT TO WITNESS THAT I, ..., DO TAKE THEE, ..., TO BE MY LAWFUL WEDDED HUSBAND, to have and to hold from this day forward, for better for worse, for richer for poorer, in sickness and in health, to love and to cherish, till death us do part, according to God's holy ordinance; and this I declare upon my honour (Salvationists add:) as a true soldier of Jesus Christ.

11. They release hands. The ring may be placed on the book. The bridegroom shall then put the ring on the appropriate finger of the bride's left hand, saying after the officiating officer:

I put this ring upon your finger as a continual sign that we are married under the solemn promises we have made this day in the name of the Father, and of the Son, and of the Holy Spirit.

If the bride is to give a ring to the bridegroom, she shall say after the officer:

I put this ring upon your finger as a continual sign that we are married under the solemn promises we have made this day in the name of the Father, and of the Son, and of the Holy Spirit.

12. The officiating officer shall join their right hands, holding them together by his own hand, and say:

In the name of God, I declare you to be husband and wife.
Whom God hath joined together, let no man put asunder.

13. The officiating officer shall then offer prayer, using

either the following words or some other suitable prayer. The couple may kneel.

> *O God our Father, giver of grace and wisdom, set your seal upon this solemn act.*
> *Give your blessing to ... and ... as they stand at the threshold of a new and holy relationship.*
> *Help them to keep the sacred promises they have made this day.*
> *Grant that they may ever love you and live in peace and harmony; and that, in all circumstances, they may seek first your Kingdom.*
> *This we ask through Jesus Christ our Lord.*
> *Amen.*

14. The officiating officer shall then end the ceremony with words such as:

> *God bless you both!*
> *God bless your family and friends!*

each of which the congregation may respond with

> *Amen.*